Also by Peter Baxter:
Rhodesia: Last Outpost of the British Empire
France in Centrafrique: From Bokassa and Operation Barracuda to the days of the EUFOR
Selous Scouts: Rhodesian Counter-Insurgency Specialists
SAAF's Border War: The South African Air Force in Combat 1966–1989
Mau Mau: Kenyan Emergency, 1952–60
Somalia: US Intervention, 1992–1994
Rhodesia Regiment, 1899–1981

Published in 2014 by:

Helion & Company Limited
26 Willow Road
Solihull
West Midlands
B91 1UE
England
Tel. 0121 705 3393
Fax 0121 711 4075
email: info@helion.co.uk
website: www.helion.co.uk

and

30° South Publishers (Pty) Ltd.
16 Ivy Road
Pinetown 3610
South Africa
email: info@30degreessouth.co.za
website: www.30degreessouth.co.za

Copyright © Peter Baxter, 2014

Designed & typeset by SA Publishing Services (kerrincocks@gmail.com)
Cover design by Kerrin Cocks

Printed and bound for Helion & Co by Henry Ling Ltd., Dorchester, Dorset and for 30° South Publishers by Pinetown Printers, Durban, South Africa

ISBN 978-1-909982-37-6

British Library Cataloguing-in-Publication Data
A catalogue record for this book is available from the British Library

Front cover: A stick commander reports back to his HQ. *Photo Rhodesian African Rifles Regimental Association (UK)*

CONTENTS

GLOSSARY

ANFO	ammonium nitrate and fuel oil explosive mixture	PATU	Police Anti-Terrorist Unit
BSAP	British South Africa Police	ter / terr	terrorist (slang)
ComOps	Combined Operations Headquarters	RAF	Royal Air Force
CT	Communist terrorist	RAR	Rhodesian African Rifles
FAF	forward airfield	RhAF	Rhodesian Air Force
FN	*Fabrique Nationale*, Belgian arms manufacturer	RIC	Rhodesian Intelligence Corps
FPLM	*Forças Populares para o Libertaçâo de Moçambique*	RLI	Rhodesian Light Infantry
Frantan	frangible tank napalm bomb	RR	Rhodesia Regiment
Frelimo	*Frente de Libertaçao de Moçambique*	RRAF	Royal Rhodesian Air Force
G-Car	Alouette III helicopter troop-carrier	RRR	Royal Rhodesia Regiment
Golf bomb	460kg Rhodesian-made pressure bomb	SAS	Special Air Service
gomo	hill (Chishona)	SB	Special Branch
JOC	Joint Operations Centre	TTL	Tribal Trust Land
K-Car	Alouette III helicopter gunship	UANC	United African National Council
MAG	*Mitrailleuse d'Appui General*, 7.62 x 51mm general-purpose machine gun	ZANLA	Zimbabwe African National Liberation Army
		ZANU	Zimbabwe African National Union
MID	Military Intelligence Directorate	ZAPU	Zimbabwe African People's Union
Mini-Golf	small version of the Golf bomb	ZIPRA	Zimbabwe People's Liberation Army
NCO	non-commissioned officer		

INTRODUCTION

On 13 September 1890, 500 men of the British South Africa Company Police stood to attention as Lieutenant Edward C. Tyndale-Biscoe ran the Union Jack up a makeshift flagpole dug into the soft earth of Mashonaland. As the ranks saluted, the first volley of a twenty-one gun salute rang across an empty landscape, and thus the birth of the British colony of Rhodesia was proclaimed.

With this display of military order complete, the men of the BSACo Police, and its associated pioneer corps—a *corps d'elite*, according to Rhodesian historian Sir Hugh Marshall-Hole, of farmers, artisans, miners, doctors, lawyers, engineers, builders, bakers, soldiers, sailors, cadets of good family with no particular occupation, cricketers, three parsons and a Jesuit—broke ranks, and for the first time since the start of the occupation, stood back to ponder the wide open country over which they now claimed control.

The British South Africa Company Pioneer Column was in fact a heavily armed, well-provisioned and independent occupation force that for several months had been probing northward from British Bechuanaland, through what would today be the southeastern lowveld of Zimbabwe, bristling with defensive capability against the not insignificant threat of attack by a shadowing force of a known 2,000 amaNdebele warriors. The entire enterprise had been extremely risky, but that risk had been obviated in part by a 10,000-candle-power searchlight that so awed the watching amaNdebele as it illuminated the surrounding bush

that an attack was never ordered. A second, and probably more authentic reason was that the amaNdebele commander-in-chief, King Lobengula, in recognition of the fact that British power had so comprehensively obliterated the Zulu nation a decade earlier, and could likewise crush the amaNdebele with similar, refused to give the order.

The Pioneer Column was a private enterprise, funded and staged by the British South Africa Company in furtherance of the imperial goals of its founder, Cecil John Rhodes, but although unofficial in this sense, there can be no doubt that the British would indeed have intervened with a large imperial force had Lobengula been so ill advised as to order an attack against the advancing agents of British imperialism.

Imperial intervention, of course, would have achieved Cecil John Rhodes's wider objective of British control of the central plateau of Mashonaland, and eventually of Matabeleland itself, but the net result would also have been *imperial* control of the territory, and not British South Africa Company control. It was essential for Rhodes to complete the occupation of Mashonaland without imperial help in order that his claim to the territory and its resources be uncomplicated by any opposing imperial claims. This was essential to keep the territory in private hands in order to satisfy the fiduciary expectations of a number of influential private investors who had supported Rhodes in this enterprise.

In the event, however, matters went precisely as planned. The Pioneer Column passed safely through Matabeleland and arrived

The Pioneer Column and men of the British South Africa Company Police, July 1890.

Illustration titled 'A Gallant Deed' depicting an 1890s BSACP patrol encountering stiff resistance from a Matabele *impi*.

Maxim guns were used to devastating effect during clashes with the Matabele during the early years of occupation.

in Mashonaland intact. Although Mashonaland at that time was a subject region of the amaNdebele, it was not strictly within amaNdebele sovereign territory. An informal frontier was then acknowledged, if not declared, between Lobengula and British South African Company administrator, Doctor Leander Starr Jameson. This followed a line along the Tokwe, Shashi and Umniati rivers that effectively separated Matabeleland from Mashonaland, but also simply deferred the glaring anomaly of an anachronistic and violently militarist African monarchy attempting to exist alongside an evolving European administration espousing the rule of law, a modern executive and an independent judiciary.

There were few among the wider British and European diasporas

in Africa at that time that grieved the obvious disadvantages of the former, although there were some that did, but very few indeed who were able to conceptualize a place in the modern world for such a system of government, and since the amaNdebele were a people defined by war, their decline would quite naturally be characterized by war. So it was in the early summer of 1893 that a pretext for war was eventually found, and a brief and bloody clash of cultures occurred between the agents of British imperialism and the last of the great African civilizations of the pre-colonial period.

The Matabele War of 1893 was a short and decisive affair that was fought over two defining battles: the battles of Bembesi and the Shangani river, and one disenchanted patrol. The circumstances of the declaration are perhaps extraneous to this account, and to some extent the conduct of the campaign itself, but it would be worth noting that the attacking forces of the British South Africa Company were made up of volunteer militias drawn from the districts of Fort Salisbury and Fort Victoria, with additional ad hoc inclusions, numbering in the hundreds, and confronting the prime of the amaNdebele military establishment which amounted to a force of upward of 15,000 men. The two battles saw various *impis*, or regiments, thrown in set-piece formations with traditional weapons, against defensive laagers armed with modern Henry-Martini rifles, Maxim guns and light artillery.

An amaNdebele defeat was somewhat inevitable, but this was made more so by a deeply conservative command element and outdated tactics that saw the human wave cut down in ranks by disciplined musketry. Had the amaNdebele been able to abandon these traditional tactics in favour of utilizing their natural and numerical advantages by harassing the advancing column in a more guerrilla style of warfare, their odds of success would have been much higher. In the event amaNdebele losses soon became unsustainable and the central cohesion of the army collapsed. On 4 November 1893, Leander Starr Jameson marched into Bulawayo at the head of a conquering force, effectively marking an end of two generations of amaNdebele monarchy in Matabeleland.

Perhaps more important, however, for the evolving Rhodesian military mindset was an episode that immediately followed the capture of Bulawayo, and this was the ill-fated Shangani Patrol, 34 members of which perished on 4 December 1893 as a consequence of competition and command anomalies pursuant to an operation launched to capture Lobengula and definitively bring an end to the war.

Leander Starr Jameson was known as a highly individualistic, impetuous and somewhat opinionated man. He was a particular favourite of Cecil John Rhodes and was given almost full discretionary power as Company Administrator of Rhodesia. This tended to reflect his position within Rhodes's organization, in which he was ubiquitous despite having no defined role or job description. Such was also the case in Rhodesia. During the conduct of the Matabele War he assumed the role of a military commander with neither military training nor any particular instinct for campaigning.

King Lobengula, commander-in-chief of the amaNdebele.

Cecil John Rhodes, founder of the British South Africa Company.

Dr Leander Starr Jameson, Rhodesian administrator of the British South Africa Company.

Major Allan Wilson, of the ill-fated Shangani Patrol.

As Company forces entered Bulawayo, by then a smoking ruin in the aftermath of its abandonment, Jameson was disappointed to discover that Lobengula himself was not waiting to offer a formal surrender, and neither was there any sign of any of the amaNdebele military commanders or any indication of the whereabouts of the bulk the of the surviving regiments. Victory could then hardly be definitively declared, although it was de facto, but this did not satisfy Jameson, who wanted either the capture of the king or clear evidence of his death.

Jameson therefore ordered a pursuit of Lobengula and his entourage north of Bulawayo and into the densely forested regions of northern Matabeleland where it was believed he had fled. Several key blunders were made in the conception and execution of this operation, most notably by Jameson himself. In the first instance, he ignored the fact that the annual rains were about to break, which would have made practical campaigning in the trackless wilds of the region, if not impossible, then certainly extremely difficult. Secondly, he ordered a column to be formed made up primarily of irregular volunteers who had been induced to fight by the promises of generous land grants and booty, both of which where there for the taking with or without the head of the king, and none of whom could see any sense in continuing the fight into the teeth of the rains when victory was to all intents and purposes theirs already. Thirdly, he made the fundamental error of placing a Sandhurst-trained, spit-and-polish product of the British Army, Major Patrick Forbes, in command of men unaccustomed to formal military discipline, and lastly, he ignored the more practical leadership experience of two irregular officers, Major Allan Wilson and Commandant Pieter Raaff, the latter an Afrikaner who had served with the British during the Anglo-Zulu War of 1879, and who knew a great deal more about the practical execution of 'native' warfare than anyone else present, both of whom Jameson placed under the command of the vastly less experienced Major Forbes.

Almost from the moment that the column marched out of Bulawayo it was beset with problems. Needless to say the rains promptly broke, after which physical conditions deteriorated

quickly and significantly. Under these circumstances, men already disinterested in the campaign and disrespectful of its commander, proved extremely difficult to motivate. Intrigues broke out between the officers, with men dividing themselves into camps and a general mood of distrust and hostility tending to pervade the whole. In the meanwhile the unbroken core of the amaNdebele army gathered on the columns flanks and shadowed it deep into the wilds of Matabeleland.

At a given point word reached the column that Lobengula was camped within striking distance. A mounted reconnaissance patrol led by Major Allan Wilson was despatched just before last light under orders to confirm the presence of Lobengula's wagons and to report back before last light. Forbes envisaged a swift dawn operation under his command to seize the king once his whereabouts had been confirmed. This was precisely what Major Wilson suspected, and in something of a clash of egos, he made the independent decision to ignore orders and remain out overnight with the 37 men of the patrol. His objective was to attempt to seize Lobengula at dawn, ostensibly in order to pre-empt Forbes doing likewise, although it would be unfair to categorically attribute his motives thus, but at the very least he was guilty of disobeying orders and of extremely risky independent action.

Overnight, under persistent rain, a large mobilization of amaNdebele forces took place, and by the time dawn broke and the patrol made ready to move it was effectively surrounded. The events thereafter have always been vague thanks to the fact that the besieged patrol was wiped out and historical accounts of the precise sequence of events have tended to be built on apocryphal oral accounts gleaned from the amaNdebele some time after the event, but glorious in the grand Victorian tradition it certainly was sufficiently maverick and individualistic to have the mark of Rhodesia written all over it.

The Shangani Patrol entered Rhodesian militarily mythology almost from the moment that the last wisps of cordite drifted off the battlefield. This would be the first and last time that a constituted native force of any sort would score such an unequivocal victory against any formal Rhodesian military formation. However, as

Major Patrick Forbes.

Commandant Pieter Raaff.

General Jan Christiaan Smuts.

General Louis Botha.

Heroic depictions of Allan Wilson and the men of the 'Shangani Patrol' during their final stand on 4 December 1893. It is said that in the killing of Wilson and his 32 men, Lobengula lost about 80 of his royal guard and another 500 or so warriors. Wilson was the last to fall as the wounded men of the patrol loaded rifles and passed them to him during the final stages of the defence. When their ammunition ran out, the remaining men of the patrol are said to have risen and sung 'God Save the Queen'. Once both of Wilson's arms were broken and he could no longer shoot, he stepped from behind a barricade of dead horses, walked toward the Matabele and was stabbed with a spear by a young warrior.

the defining myth of Rhodesian military conduct, the Shangani Patrol would not be the last time that Rhodesian men in uniform would buck the rules and go for broke in a manner that would both gain the respect and provoke the despair of more orthodox military commanders among the various imperial formations that Rhodesians served in, or were associated with, during the three major conflicts of the twentieth century.

The Matabele War of 1893 was followed three years later by an uprising known variously as the Matabele Rebellion or the Second Matabele War. This was conducted in largely un-associated parallel with a concurrent rebellion launched by the Mashona tribes of the central plateau region known as Mashonaland, and again variously termed the Mashona Rebellion or the First *Chimurenga*.* The colonial response to this was at first ad hoc and rather hastily configured, but very soon a series of emergency responses coalesced into the first formally organized local militias, followed by a large-scale imperial intervention conducted on formal and professional military lines. Efforts to trace Rhodesian military history have always tended to be disunited over the question of whether the Rhodesian army as an institution began with the

formation of the British South Africa Company Police in 1890, the raising of militias during the First Matabele War, and likewise the Second Matabele War, or indeed as a response to the need for imperial defence during the Anglo-Boer War of 1899–1902 when the first reference to the Rhodesia regiment was made.

The Rhodesia regiment was first mooted as a formal military unit in August 1899 upon the arrival in Bulawayo of the much-storied Colonel Robert Baden-Powell who had been ordered by the War Office to raise two regiments from local manpower resources in order to protect the southern flanks of the empire against any aggressive intent from the Boers of the Transvaal. The first of these was the Rhodesia regiment and the second the Protectorate regiment, the first, as the name suggests, pertaining to Rhodesia, and the second pertaining to the Bechuanaland Protectorate where it served. The use of a lowercase 'r' in the regimental title of both of these units implies that neither had the title of regiment, but that each was simply identified as a regiment with specific origins.

In this regard, therefore, it becomes difficult to link the Rhodesia regiment of the Anglo-Boer War as the progenitor the more formally organized battalions of the Rhodesia Regiment that were established for service in German South West Africa and German

* *Chimurenga*: revolutionary war, revolutionary struggle or war of liberation.

The Matabele Rebellion: defences at Bulawayo during the uprising of 1896.

1st Battalion, Rhodesia Regiment camped under the Erongo mountains in German South West Africa, 1915. *Source Charlie Aust*

1st Battalion, Rhodesia Regiment, 4.7-inch naval guns in action at Karub in German South West Africa, 1915. *Source Charlie Aust*

East Africa during the First World War. This regiment had more in common with the orthodox organizational mores of the British Army, the model of all substantial imperial armed formations and the mark of a unit representing an army proper.

The 1st Battalion, Rhodesia Regiment, was formed for service as part of a larger South African contingent earmarked to deal with clearing the Germans out of what was then German South West Africa. The broad strategic rationale for this was the fear of German access to the deepwater port of Walvis Bay. A brilliant mechanized and mounted desert campaign was conceived and executed by South African prime minister General Louis Botha and his aide-de-camp General Jan Christiaan Smuts that achieved its objective with a minimum of actual combat but a significant amount of manoeuvre and battlefield engineering. The 1st Battalion of the Rhodesia Regiment followed in the dust of advancing South African units, playing for the most part a garrison role, and dying of frustration and disappointment after the campaign as Rhodesians decamped in droves in order to sign up with other British imperial units for more guaranteed action on the Western Front.

It is interesting to note here that en route to Britain the first contingent of Rhodesian men destined for the British Army, led by a certain Captain Brady, where seconded into the King's Royal Rifle Corps, forming a Rhodesian platoon that survived,

albeit under great pressure, until the end of the war, forming a fraternal bond between the Rhodesia Regiment and the KRRC that endures in spirit to this day.

In the meanwhile the demise of the 1st Battalion was followed soon afterward by the formation of the 2nd Battalion for service in German East Africa. There are many among the strong fraternity of Rhodesian military historians who claim this to be arguably the most evocative and celebrated phase of Rhodesian military history. It certainly proved the mettle of Rhodesian fighting men, and was the first independent, locally commanded Rhodesian unit to gain significant combat experience on a foreign field of battle.

The East African Campaign of the First World War was the most enduring single operation of the war, commencing with the outbreak of hostilities in August 1914 and continuing for several months beyond the armistice with no conclusive result besides a general surrender concurrent with the wider results of the war. In truth it might easily have continued into perpetuity as one of the first true modern guerrilla campaigns to be fought in any twentieth-century theatre.

The campaign was executed on the Allied side by arguably one of the world's great virtuosos of guerrilla warfare, the polymath soldier-statesman General Jan Christiaan Smuts, even a cursory biography of whom would consume more pages allocated for this entire volume, and likewise his opposing commander, Colonel Paul von Lettow-Vorbeck, who conceived and conducted a campaign to frustrate and preoccupy vast numbers of Allied troops and to direct colossal amounts of military ordnance away from the Western Front in order to aide the German effort, and based largely on the understanding that what was lost in Africa would be reclaimed several times over once the Axis powers had claimed final victory over the Allies in Europe.

History, of course, frustrated this aim, but not in any way to detract from the sheer brilliance of both men, neither of whom was able to claim substantive victory over the other, and both of whom became great admirers of one another in later years, and almost tentative friends.

A secondary point here is that once the Rhodesia Regiment had been removed from the East African theatre, in the spring of 1917, the conclusion had been reached, thanks to the sheer numbers of

Colonel Algernon Essex Capell reviews his troops on the march, East Africa campaign, 1916.

Men of the 1st Rhodesia Native Regiment march through the streets of the Southern Rhodesian capital, Salisbury in 1916, prior to going to war in East Africa.

men succumbing to tropical disease in East Africa, some thirty men for every battlefield casualty, that the use of white men as field troops in an African theatre was a recipe for suicide. As a consequence the Rhodesia Native Regiment was formed, and it was this that replaced white Rhodesian manpower on the frontline for the concluding phases of the East Africa Campaign.

The 2nd Battalion of the Rhodesia Regiment was disbanded soon after its return from East Africa, dying largely of depletion, but the Rhodesia Native Regiment survived the war, the two battalions of which were merged with the Matabeleland Native Regiment to form a single Rhodesian Native Regiment battalion, the first permanent regular unit of the Rhodesian Army to be formed.

The loss of the two territorial battalions of the Rhodesia Regiment was not permanent. As the colony of Rhodesia matured, and as more substantial institutions of state evolved, so the local territorial force became a permanent feature of the colony with the gazetting of the Defence Act in 1926 that made provision for the establishment of a permanent territorial force in the form of two territorial battalions and a cadet corps. A certain Captain Hugo Watson was seconded to Southern Rhodesia on assignment from the War Office to organize the colony's defences along lines that would endure until the collapse of Rhodesia in 1980.

The Rhodesia Regiment, therefore, returned into being and remained a feature of the Rhodesian defence establishment for the remainder of the life of the colony. It was suspended briefly for the period of the Second World War in respect of the fact that Rhodesian military personnel were in the main so highly regarded that concentrating them in a single formation would be counterproductive to other units requiring senior NCO and commissioned officers of a very high calibre, and also in respect of lessons learned during the First World War where so much of the white manpower resources of a small colony had been decimated through service in a single battalion.[*]

---

[*] Rhodesian military history is replete with references to the high quality of Rhodesian servicemen. This has been attributed variously to the high standards of immigration applicable to Rhodesia in the early days, the ability of almost all white males in Africa to shoot and ride and the fact that growing up on farms with large black labour forces accustomed Rhodesian youth to command and man-management from an early age.

The regiment was re-formed after the Second World War with the battle honours of the Second World War added to East Africa, South West Africa and the Anglo-Boer War, with the additional honour in 1947 of King George VI consenting to be commander-in-chief, allowing for the addition of a royal prefix to the regimental title, after which the Royal Rhodesia Regiment found official favour and a great deal of respect.

Sadly, after the Second World War, this high-water mark of imperial relations began to decline. If the First World War weakened the knees of European empire, the Second World War laid it on the canvas. The granting of independence to India in 1947 set the tone for a domino effect of collapse across the spectrum of British overseas territories. The granting of independence to Gold Coast in 1957 began the process in Africa, followed by Nigeria, Sierra Leone, Gambia and the rest of British West Africa. Kenya was granted independence in 1963, followed by Nyasaland and Northern Rhodesia, both in 1964, all of which sent shockwaves through the remaining regions of white Africa, most notably Rhodesia, South West Africa and South Africa. The granting of independence to the Belgian Congo in June 1960, with the rapid descent onto total anarchy that followed, appeared to confirm to many whites concentrated south of the Zambezi that any similar concession to black majority rule in their territories would result in the same levels of maniacal warfare and internecine bloodshed, and a deep-rooted sense of determination to avoid this fate manifested itself in a radical swing to the right, and an arming for war that to all but the most determinedly blind appeared absolutely inevitable.

At the same time Britain entered into a phase of existence that many, both then and now, reflect back upon as being less than her finest hour. The intensely moralistic and economically moribund post-war years sent many a demobilized soldier and his family to the colonies, and indeed the white population of Rhodesia reached its all-time high during the 1950s, peaking at some 260,000 souls. Many felt they owed little loyalty to Britain, and were dismayed as the successive Labour governments of Attlee and Wilson, and the weak Conservative governments in between, were seen to be eroding the moral stature of empire and sliding into appeasement

General Paul von Lettow-Vorbeck.
Source www.feldgrau.net

British Prime Minister Harold Macmillan.

Frelimo troops in action. *Source Times Media*

while displaying an unseemly willingness to sacrifice the lives and livelihoods of their citizens overseas to a repulsively zealous wave of black liberation.

This, of course, is a gross over-simplification of the facts. The African liberation movement had by then come of age, and white government in Africa had become a manifest anachronism, but the problem of incumbent white populations in the settled colonies remained a conundrum with no easy or obvious answer.

Rhodesian Prime Minister Ian Douglas Smith.

Following independence in June 1975, Frelimo sought to transform its guerrilla forces into a conventional army with Soviet and Eastern Bloc assistance to counter the Rhodesian and South African military threat. *Source Centro de Formação Fotográfica, Maputo, Mozambique*

The British political establishment might have been privately sympathetic to the plight of white Rhodesians, but at that point in history there was very little that could be practically done about it. Winston Churchill had placed his signature on the Atlantic Charter in part as a means to secure US support during the Second World War, and the tenets of self-determination for all espoused in that document sat very comfortably with the post-war rise of nationalist politics worldwide.

In Rhodesia things were no different. The late 1950s and early 1960s where characterized by the emergence of a corps of highly educated and deeply politicized young blacks who where critical of their parents' collaborationist relationship with the whites. They tended toward the view that the whites could leave the continent at their earliest convenience and take their elitist political institutions with them. *One man one vote* became the mantra, and from a purely moral perspective this was a difficult demand to deny. Popular discontent was harnessed into mass movements: unions and pressure groups emerged as political parties, charismatic leadership found fruitful voice, and before too long the surviving white governments of southern Africa found themselves confronted by situations bordering on social anarchy.

The first shots fired in the southern chapter of the African liberation struggle were in the Portuguese territories of Angola

and Mozambique, the former in 1961 and the latter 1964. It is worth noting that the Portuguese had a very different attitude to the colonial experience in Africa than the British, which by the 1960s was the only European power, other than the Portuguese, still ostensibly active in sub-Saharan Africa. While British prime minister Harold Macmillan was attempting to prime Britain's African territories with the inevitability of decolonization, Portugal's somewhat anachronistic fascist dictatorship remained determined to retain control of what were termed Overseas Provinces for the sake of waning national prestige.

The war of independence in Angola began as a relatively low-key and containable insurgency involving three major liberation movements, but devolved as the 1970s dawned into a much more serious civil war, escalating further in the 1980s into a multi-faceted Cold War engagement. The Angolan Civil War, which merged with the South African Border War, ultimately sucked South Africa, Angola, Cuba and the Soviet Union into a bloody contest that featured a number of conventional armoured battles on a scale not seen since the North African Campaign of the Second World War.

The Mozambican war of liberation was somewhat less of an open breach, and was fought on more classically configured counter-insurgency lines between the Portuguese armed forces and a single, unified liberation movement known as the *Frente*

Portuguese troops arrive in Luanda, Angola.
Source The Argus Printing and Publishing Co (Pty) Ltd

de Libertação de Moçambique, or Frelimo, operating initially out of forward bases in southern Tanzania, and later, as territorial gains were made, from within the Tete province of Mozambique itself.

The proximity of Mozambique and Rhodesia, and the long common frontier between the two territories, and of course the long-standing mutual trade and transport dependencies, tended to render Rhodesia deeply invested in the outcome and prosecution of the war in Mozambique, even though official military cooperation tended to be low key and limited. Nonetheless, the advent of war in Mozambique signalled a commencement of war in Rhodesia, and indeed it was from 1964 onward that Rhodesian military, intelligence and security personnel were involved in what could be termed an armed and organized civil war.

In 1964, however, Rhodesia was still a de facto British colony, and although the security situation throughout the sub-continent spoke very loudly of war, political manoeuvres tended to eclipse military preparations as a new paradigm approached.

The background to this is important in understanding the subsequent dynamics of the Rhodesian civil war and the circumstances under which it was fought. As mentioned earlier, events north of the Zambezi, in particular the anarchic explosion of violence that immediately followed independence in the Belgian Congo, tended to convince white Rhodesia that any concession to local demands for majority rule would see an immediate replication of Congo in Rhodesia, which at all costs had to be avoided. A relatively moderate territorial government in Rhodesia was replaced in 1964, upon the collapse of the short-lived Federation of Rhodesia and Nyasaland, by a hard-line, right-wing government led by dogmatic Prime Minister Ian Douglas Smith.*

Two key actions followed the achievement of power of the Rhodesia Front in the 1964 general election in Rhodesia. The first was the introduction of a State of Emergency that remained in place throughout the remaining life of the colony. It facilitated the banning and outlawing of all local black nationalist political parties—ZANU (Zimbabwe African National Union) and ZAPU (Zimbabwe African People's Union)—and the detention, imprisonment or restriction of the entire spectrum of senior black political leadership.

The net effect of this was to bring to a rapid end the seething political unrest that had plagued the colony since the late 1950s, but it also sent a clear message to those black political leaders detained within the country, and those that had been spared or had escaped detention, and who then left Rhodesia to form committees in exile in newly independent Zambia, that simple civil unrest and civil disobedience alone would not achieve independence in Rhodesia, as it had elsewhere on the continent. War was now inevitable, and as a consequence committees of war were formed, foreign assistance sought and proto-armed organizations formed with the express purpose of initiating an armed confrontation with the forces of white Rhodesia.

Again, this is something of an over-simplification of the facts, but in broad brushstrokes it defines the circumstances under which the seeds of war in the region were sown. The second significant action undertaken by the Rhodesian Front government soon after taking over power was to pick a fight with the British over the question of minority-rule independence from Britain, a clear impossibility under the circumstances, in order to bring the matter of the long-term future of Rhodesia to a head for better or for worse.† The effect of this was a very public squabble between Rhodesian prime minister Ian Douglas Smith and British prime minister Harold Wilson, which, against a backdrop of palpable personal animosity, resulted in a Unilateral Declaration of Independence from Britain by Rhodesia on 11 November 1965, an event known as UDI. This effectively severed all relations between Britain and her erstwhile colony, bringing upon the rebel colony a condition of international sanctions and rendering war inevitable without the possibility of any direct aid or intervention from Britain. The stage was set.

---

* The Federation of Rhodesia and Nyasaland, or the Central African Federation, was an attempt by all three surviving British territories in southern Africa—Southern and Northern Rhodesia and Nyasaland—to federate in an effort to fend of the looming inevitability of decolonization in the region. It survived from 1953 to 1963 and collapsed as a consequence of nationalist activity, first in Nyasaland and then Northern Rhodesia, both of which achieved independence in 1964 as Malawi and Zambia respectively.

† A feature of the preamble of the Federal constitution had been that upon secession from the Federation each territory would be granted independence. Nyasaland and Northern Rhodesia had been granted independence under a majority-rule constitution, and as a consequence of this white Rhodesia held out for independence from Britain under the terms of minority rule. Whatever might have been the hopes and expectations of white Rhodesia, at this point minority rule was politically impossible and as such was quite obviously a fallacious demand by the right-wing government of Ian Smith.

CHAPTER ONE:
THE PLAYERS

Britain was faced with two colonial rebellions in the immediate aftermath of the Second World War. The first was the Malayan Emergency and the second the Mau Mau Uprising in Kenya. Mau Mau was a curiously atavistic affair focused primarily in the Central Highlands of Kenya and was dealt with as a civil disturbance with local and imperial military forces used primarily in support of the civil power. Malaya was also treated as a civil disturbance, mainly in order to avoid the awkward classification of a war, but it required a more concentrated military involvement, and it was indeed here that many established British counter-insurgency tactics were established.

At about the same time that the Malayan Emergency erupted, the Korean War broke out, which created a demand for a Commonwealth contingent to assist United Nations forces made up primarily of Americans. A small force of 100 men was raised in Rhodesia for service in Korea, but were diverted to Malaya at the last minute where they became known as C Squadron SAS (Malayan Scouts). This was something of a continuation of the Rhodesian dominated C Squadron SAS that saw service during the desert campaign of the Second World War, and later became the basis of the Rhodesian C Squadron SAS. C Squadron (Rhodesia) SAS was formally reconstituted in 1962 as the main offensive arm of the Rhodesian Army that prior to this had consisted of only an enlarged Rhodesia Regiment that at its height would comprise eight battalions, and initially one, but later two battalions of the Rhodesian African Rifles.

In addition to this the British South Africa Police retained some of its early paramilitary capacity, and remained the formal first line of defence of the nation until the first substantive clash of arms on 28 April 1966, when a small detachment of Zimbabwe African National Liberation Army (ZANLA) forces was annihilated by a combined police and air force operation. The BSAP retained a substantial reserve force that assumed a more direct paramilitary role during the war, alongside a significant contingent of black servicemen and a Support Unit with full combat capabilities.

The Rhodesian Air Force (RhAF) owed its origins to the Royal Air Force, or indeed, further back in history than this, to an Air Wing of the Rhodesia Regiment incorporated in 1935. Much of the hardware that would sustain it through the darkest days of the war was allocated to Southern Rhodesia as part of the dispensation of Federal assets when the Federation of Rhodesia and Nyasaland collapsed. These included a squadron of Hawker Hunter strike jets, a squadron of English Electric Canberra light bombers and the ubiquitous Alouette III helicopters that would form the backbone of the Rhodesian counter-insurgency response until 1980.

Besides this, during the period between the gazetting of the Defence Act in 1926 and the outbreak of civil war in 1964, a variety

C Squadron SAS (Malayan Scouts) in the jungle on a rafting patrol (note the 68lb troop radio on the soldier's back).

Ron Reid-Daly as a sergeant (bearded, bush hat turned up) in jovial mood in Malaya. He has just returned from a three-month operation in the jungle.

Sergeant Billy Conn, C Squadron SAS radio operator, in a Malayan paddy field. He is reporting to the aircraft that all is well on the DZ after an operational parachute deployment.

A patrol of Rhodesian African Rifles navigates the Pagoh swamp in Malaya. *Source Masodja*

A 'dryish' patch in the Pagoh swamp. *Source Masodja*

of additional units were formed, including engineers, signals, armoured car and artillery regiments, and then, in 1961, a light infantry battalion, the much-storied Rhodesian Light Infantry. Later, as the war progressed, a specialized BSAP reserve unit known as the Police Anti-Terrorist Unit, formed in 1964, assumed the role of a localized hunter–killer formation configured to utilize local knowledge in the isolated rural areas of Rhodesia to monitor, track and destroy infiltrating guerrilla groups.

Perhaps the most eclectic unit within a generally innovative and creative military establishment was a mounted infantry regiment known as the Grey's Scouts, after a fabled Rhodesian commando rider, Sir George Grey, whose fame was derived from his exploits during the Second Matabele War of 1896. It was not until 1976, however, that arguably the most recognizable special force unit in the Rhodesian stable was formed, the Selous Scouts.

The Selous Scouts was formed at its nucleus as a psuedo-operations unit. The concept of the regiment was informed by the need for relevant, up-to-date intelligence on the movement of guerrilla units through the native reserves and tribal trust lands. A certain amount of false mythology exists regarding the role of white operatives in the Selous Scouts. Very rarely did white operatives seriously attempt to pass themselves off in operational conditions as authentic guerrillas utilizing elaborate make-up and a fluency in African languages.

This was largely a myth. In fact the majority of pseudo operators were turned guerrillas, with white operatives tending to be handlers rather than frontline personnel, and indeed many men who passed the rigorous Selous Scouts selection, and were deployed as pseudo handlers, left the regiment in search of more guaranteed action elsewhere. White Selous Scouts members very often found themselves located on observations posts (OPs) directing the operations of black pseudo groups engaged in the actual infiltration of guerrilla bands. After 1976, as the Selous Scouts became more involved in hot-pursuit and cross-border offensive operations in Mozambique and Zambia, operations which required more orthodox infantry contributions, a great deal more action could be guaranteed by association with the Selous Scouts, and much of the reputation of the regiment as it has endured in the years since is based on this period, and this style of operation. While these more high-profile operations were underway, the pseudo element of the Selous Scouts continued to function extremely effectively, and indeed there are many who were once associated with the regiment who believe that this was the core and nexus of the Selous Scouts ethos, and the more infantry-oriented membership an unwanted and unwarranted gung-ho extension.

Be that as it may, the Selous Scouts was arguably one of the most successful manifestations of force in the Rhodesian Army, and through both its intelligence-gathering arm and its hard-hitting pseudo column and reconnaissance operations, it accounted for the greater part of the Rhodesian success in the hard fighting years between 1976 and 1980.

The glue that bound together the various arms of the Rhodesian security forces was the two key intelligence arms, the Central Intelligence Organization, formed in 1963 under the leadership of the enigmatic and highly mercurial Rhodesian intelligence supremo Ken Flower, and Special Branch, a police intelligence agency modelled on the similar British and Commonwealth internal security organs concerned specifically with local intelligence matters. The former organization tended to concentrated on external intelligence liaison and operations, and so did not have the same impact on the direct prosecution of the war as Special Branch, which was a phenomenally successful organization, accounting for the complete annihilation of initial hostile incursions into Rhodesia, and later during the war, fine-tuning itself into arguably one of the most exceptional organizations of its type in the world at that time.

The horizontal rope on the selection assault course at Wafa Wafa training camp, Kariba. The 34-foot drop is into thorn bush.

A large number of Selous Scouts pseudo operators were turned guerrillas; here a soldier prepares to deploy.

Selous Scouts cross-border offensive operation.

So much for Rhodesian force. On the nationalist side matters progressed in a manner less orthodox but no less committed.

There were two major nationalist organizations in existence in 1964–5 as white Rhodesia grasped the raw facts of war and armed herself to confront it. These were ZAPU and ZANU. The former was the senior party which owed its origins to the formation in 1934 of the Southern Rhodesia Bantu Congress, which transmuted in 1957 to the Southern Rhodesia African National Congress under the leadership of local nationalist Joshua Nkomo, further reinventing itself, upon the banning of the Southern Rhodesia ANC, as the National Democratic Party (NDP), finally emerging as the Zimbabwe African People's Union in 1961, again as a consequence of the banning of the NDP.

ZANU emerged as a splinter group of ZAPU, harnessing arguably the most talented leadership of the latter in a breakaway formation that initially lacked eligibility, but ultimately emerged as the more powerful and dynamically led of the two organizations.

Joshua Nkomo was a large, comfort-loving and somewhat venal character who seemed to always manage to be absent from Rhodesia when the worst of fortunes befell his fellow nationalists. He was without doubt an authentic product of the period, and certainly a pedigreed nationalist, but he was also prone to the comforts of his position and less enamoured with its rigours. As a consequence he lost the respect and support of an up-and-coming generation of powerfully motivated and intensely politicized newcomers led by the ferociously intellectual and fearlessly ascetic Robert Mugabe.

Matters came to a head in 1964 when Joshua Nkomo persuaded his fellow, and somewhat more radical, members of ZAPU to quit Rhodesia in favour of a governing committee abroad, based in Dar es Salaam, and according to Nkomo, based on an invitation from then Tanzanian president Julius Nyerere. In the event it was discovered that Nyerere had offered no such invitation, and moreover publicaly rebuked Nkomo for his manifest unwillingness to punch it out in the trenches of African nationalism within Rhodesia, and to accept incarceration as an inevitable by-product of his stated political commitment.

Nkomo returned somewhat meekly to Rhodesia and stepped obediently into his corner to fight the good fight, but by then it was too late. A clique of those who had followed him to Tanzania—Mugabe, of course, but also a qualified barrister by the name of Herbert Chitepo, and a somewhat less dynamic but senior nationalist by the name of Ndabaningi Sithole—formed a breakaway faction known as the Zimbabwe African National Union (ZANU). This, to the absolute delight of the Rhodesian authorities, prompted a murderous bout of internecine violence that consumed both parties and accounted for a great deal of the insecurity and violence that wracked the townships of Rhodesia through 1964–5.

That notwithstanding, when the bannings arrived after the ascension to power in Rhodesia of the Rhodesian Front, all parties and national leaders were subject to the same terms of arrest and detention, and while the luminaries of the struggle languished in prisons and detention camps across Rhodesia, their various deputies and leadership committees decamped to Lusaka, the Zambian capital, where concentrated thought began to be given to the formation of armies.

CIO's Ken Flower.

ZAPU's Joshua Nkomo.

ZANU's Ndabaningi Sithole.

ZANU's Herbert Chitepo.

The first among equals in this regard was ZANU. The main substantive leadership bloc of ZANU, including Ndabaningi Sithole, the elected leader of ZANU, and Robert Mugabe, the de facto leader, were detained at Sikombela Detention Centre near Gokwe. Here a meeting was held to discuss the rather gloomy state of affairs confronting the liberation movement in Rhodesia, which led to the epoch-making appreciation that armed resistance had now become inevitable. A declaration known as the *Sikombela* Declaration was drafted which authorized the ZANU leadership in exile, headed by Herbert Chitepo to form a council of war, the *Dare re Chimurenga*, to which would be appended a revolutionary council and guerrilla army.*

The exiled leadership of ZAPU, in the meanwhile, under the relatively pedestrian leadership of veteran nationalist James Chikerema, established a Special Affairs desk similarly charged with the responsibility of forming, training and arming a guerrilla force.

The dichotomy here is an interesting one. ZAPU was the senior organization, and so enjoyed the support of the Frontline States, a grouping of liberated states adjacent to Rhodesia: Mozambique and Angola, where the three main flashpoints of the liberation struggle existed, which tended to place ZAPU in a position to receive higher levels of arms, training and support than were available to ZANU. ZANU remained cast as a splinter group that had compromised the unity of the combined liberation movement, and was forced to fall back on its own resources in the matter of the recruitment, training and arming of its revolutionary cadres.

Despite this, the pace at which ZAPU went about the process of building an armed wing did not compare to the revolutionary zeal of ZANU, then under the dynamic and forward-thinking leadership of arguably one of the most worthwhile players in the liberation drama, Herbert Chitepo. Chitepo was a barrister and the first black member of the Rhodesian Bar. He had suffered the various pinpricks of petty racism that all blacks in southern Africa were subject to on one level or another, but he had never been imprisoned, never been detained, and as such did not harbour the animosity toward the system that many others in the leadership did. He was intelligent, erudite, pragmatic and relatively moderate, and moreover, having served briefly as Tanzanian Director of

Public Prosecutions, he was well connected in Tanzania. This helped in his efforts to source funds and training facilities in Tanzania, where the first intake of recruits was directed for military training.

ZAPU enjoyed membership of a club regarded as authentic national liberation movements, recognized by the Organization of African Unity and the Frontline States alongside other pedigreed organizations such as the South African ANC, South West Africa's SWAPO, Frelimo and the MPLA. These organizations also enjoyed the support of the Soviet Union and other Eastern Bloc countries, presenting enhanced opportunities for arms supplies and overseas training, which ZAPU availed itself to.

While both organizations worked to establish their armed wings, white Rhodesia languished in a certain amount of complacency. The banning of all nationalist political parties and the detention and restriction of all the leading nationalists neutered the violence that had wracked the territory in the run-up to UDI, leaving the government to concentrate on the ongoing settlement negotiations with the British government, and for white Rhodesia in general to congratulate itself on standing up to the spinelessness of the British and ostensibly winning.

International sanctions had been declared almost immediately after the declaration of independence, but these were rolled out incrementally which allowed the Rhodesians to put in place alternative and circuitous supply channels for fuel and armaments as well as all other necessary imports, while at the same time forging new and lucrative markets for Rhodesian raw materials and agricultural products. Portugal, in respect of its own civil wars in Mozambique and Angola, did not openly flout international sanctions, but it certainly did not comply, and in fact Rhodesian fuel imports enriched many Portuguese businessmen, quite as it did many Rhodesian businessmen.

Rhodesia, therefore, became dependent on her two key neighbours, Mozambique and South Africa, and in the short term survived the imposition of sanctions very well. The long-term inevitability of war, however, remained as much a fact of life then as ever, although it appeared that only a few well-placed internal security agents seemed prepared to acknowledge this, and one or two white liberals, none of whom found their voices particularly popular, and white Rhodesia sailed forth almost universally oblivious to the dark storm clouds gathering on the horizon.

---

* Council of War, in chiShona *dare* [dah-rare] meaning a meeting of senior figures and *chimurenga* meaning war, or struggle.

CHAPTER TWO:
THE FIRST SHOTS

The first ZANLA training base was established at the site of an old German gold mine known as Itumbi Reefs which was situated close to the southern Tanzania town of Mbeya. Here an initial intake of 24 men undertook basic and somewhat rudimentary guerrilla training. Later, twenty graduates were summoned to ZANU headquarter in Lusaka for a briefing on their first mission.

This envisaged a coordinated operation planned to utilize four groups of five men each, each designated a specific operational sector. The first group, codenamed Chimurenga, was ordered to makes its way to the Eastern Highlands of Rhodesia with the objective of sabotaging the Feruka oil refinery and its lengthy pipeline located some eighteen kilometres outside the border city of Umtali. The second group, codenamed Demolition, was allocated the Fort Victoria district as its theatre of operations where its orders were general: to destroy bridges and culverts on the road between Fort Victoria and Beitbridge. The third group, codenamed Gukule-Honde, was given the less-offensive task of penetrating the highly politicized Zvimba District, northwest of the capital Salisbury, with orders to subvert the local population. Thereafter it was to be joined by the fourth group, codenamed Armageddon, to recruit and conduct military training while also attacking any targets of opportunity in the surrounding districts.

The combined group crossed into Rhodesia from Zambia on 1 and 2 April 1966, breaching the Zambezi river before breaking up and each heading toward their designated sectors. Things began to unravel very quickly though as the first group, Chimurenga, alerted the local population to their arrival almost immediately, and were arrested in Old Umtali within hours of their arrival. Under interrogation the full scope of the combined operation was revealed, resulting in the rolling out of a Rhodesian security operation codenamed Pagoda I and Pagoda II, which effectively marked the beginning of the shooting war in Rhodesia.*

Demolition was identified and dealt with fairly quickly as a police action with no specific military involvement. Armageddon remained at large for much longer. In the interim one desultory sabotage attempt was made against the Chirundu–Makuti road and another against a police station, with a further attempt made to destroy an electricity pylon near Alaska Mine. Soon afterward

---

* There has always been dispute between ZANU and ZAPU as to who fired the first shots in the Zimbabwe-Rhodesia war of liberation. One of the first identifiable guerrilla actions perpetrated by a ZAPU guerrilla unit was an attack in September 1964 on the homestead of Dube Ranch in the Kezi farming district some 40 miles south of Bulawayo. The attack was brief and ineffectual and was abandoned quickly with the combatants leaving most of their weaponry at the scene and fleeing west across the border into Bechianaland (which became Botswana in 1966) where they were soon arrested and handed back to Rhodesian authorities. This might be construed as the opening act of the Rhodesian war, but the 'Battle of Sinoia', consequent to the actions described above, is generally accepted as the point at which the war commenced.

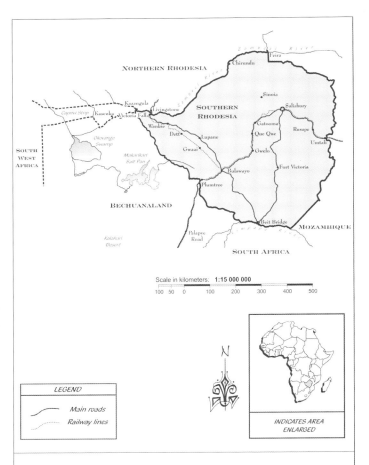

SOUTHERN RHODESIA

Source Genevieve Edwards

the group went to ground on a property near Sinoia that was owned by farmer Noel Edwards. Here they were quickly noticed by local black residents and their presence reported to the police.

There have been many different accounts of what happened next, and the importance of what did happen is mainly in the effect it had on the future operational methodology of the combined Rhodesian security forces in the aftermath. According to Rhodesian intelligence chief Ken Flower, who wrote a detailed account of the episode in his autobiography, *Serving Secretly*, the reporting of the presence of the guerrilla groups in the Sinoia area was not the first notification the authorities had received. Flower states that the group had in fact been under observation for some time, but since they did not at that moment represent any particular security threat, it was deemed logical simply to keep them under observation in order to see what further intelligence they could provide—and certainly, at a time when intelligence was more important than operational kills, there would be nothing to be gained by making martyrs of the men.

A combined forces patrol in the Zambezi valley in the mid-1960s when early insurgency groups began infiltrating across the river.

Operations Centre (JOC) under which the war would be fought from that point on.

As Ken Flower had predicted, an unintended corollary of this action was the regional, and perhaps international, lionization of the heroes of the battle, the ZANLA cadres, who could certainly not be accused of anything other than dying in battle with great courage. The men of the Armageddon group were immediately hailed as liberation heroes, and the action celebrated as the Battle of Sinoia, or Chinhoyi as it became after independence, and the day, 28 April, commemorated as Chimurenga Day. Perhaps more importantly at the time was that the incident symbolized the coming of age of ZANU as a political party, ZANLA as a military formation and the fact that this particular faction of the liberation fraternity had fired the first shots in the Zimbabwe–Rhodesia civil war.

The Sinoia incident did not mark the end of Operation Pagoda. For several weeks the six-man Gukule-Honde group remained at large until their location was confirmed by the murder on Tuesday morning, 17 May 1966, of local white farmer Johannes Viljoen, who was gunned down alongside his wife after he responded to a knock at the door of his Nevada Farm homestead, located a few miles north of Hartley, some sixty miles west of Salisbury. An unsuccessful follow-up was conducted by units of the Rhodesian Light Infantry. A week later a combined army and police patrol, acting on information received, shot and wounded one insurgent, killing a second the following day. Thereafter no further contact was made and on 21 June 1966 troops were withdrawn and Operation Pagoda I officially curtailed.

The four surviving members of the fugitive group managed to make their way undetected as far as Kanyemba on the south bank of the Zambezi river within striking distance of safety when they attracted the attention of a local district messenger who alerted the local police member-in-charge. Also based at the Kanyemba police station at that time was a detachment of 1RAR which immediately mounted a follow-up which resulted in a brief but unsuccessful contact. The incident was reported back to Salisbury and Operation Pagoda II swung into action. The body of one insurgent was found in the contact area but it was not until November 1966 that the remaining three were accounted for. One slipped into Mozambique and was detained by the Portuguese, while the other two were arrested in Mtoko and Mount Hampden.

In the meanwhile, as ongoing mopping-up operations associated with Operation Pagoda were still underway, the first substantial ZAPU military operations took place. On 16 July 1966 two ZAPU groups of five and six men respectively successfully crossed the Zambezi river a short distance downstream of Kanyemba and attempted to infiltrate the country; unfortunately they became entangled in the follow-up conducted against survivors of Gukule-Honde, and were accounted for relatively quickly.

Popular mythology then goes on to indicate that commissioner of police Frank Barfoot insisted that the British South Africa Police, as the agency traditionally responsible for internal security, was solely responsible for dealing with the issue as a police matter. Alexandre Binda, Rhodesian military historian and author of several books on the subject, states that, without consultation, the police then mounted an operation against the Armageddon group using 83 policemen, 39 of whom were reservists, supported by four Royal Rhodesian Air Force helicopters, one of which was armed with a mounted 7.62mm machine gun.

Using a collection of outdated weapons, including early Second World War Sten sub-machine guns, obsolete Lee-Enfield .303s and Greener single-shot shotguns, the Rhodesians faced down a small group of resolute guerrillas armed with modern automatic assault rifles, and dealt with the entire group relatively easily. The inter-service fall-out of the operation, however, was less easily resolved.

Immediately after the operation an Operations Coordinating Committee meeting was held that saw accusations and counter-accusations of bad faith flying across the table.* What emerged, however, was an agreement that, should any incident fall beyond the control of any single service, it would be dealt with by the combined capacity of all branches of the security forces. Some suggested that this would mean the BSAP would be obliged to seek the assistance of the army as and when it deemed the situation required it, but others, Ken Flower among them, stated that it was in fact a trimming of the wide prerogative previously enjoyed by the BSAP as the nation's first line of defence. Whatever might have been the case, the incident brought into being the Joint

---

* The Operations Coordinating Committee (OCC) was a war council of sorts, established in 1964 with the responsibility of coordinating combined operations. It consisted of the heads of services: army, air force and police—and Director General of the CIO, which, throughout its existence as an arm of Rhodesian intelligence, was Ken Flower.

Operation Grampus: six terrorists kneel in front of PWO Wurayayi's patrol. Note that three of them are armed with PPSh sub-machine guns and three with SKS assault rifles. This gave them far greater fire power than the five SLRs carried by this 1RAR patrol. *Source Masodja*

Operation Grampus: members of the BSAP are called in by the patrol to search the prisoners. *Source Masodja*

The next ZAPU incursion was no less fraught. Two six-man groups crossed the Zambezi river southwest of Lake Kariba under orders to infiltrate into the Nkai and Gwelo–Que Que areas. This required an overland penetration through an area that was ostensibly a grassroots ZAPU support base, but the loyalty and commitment of the general African population to the struggle could not at that point be guaranteed. The general mission was to set up base camps for the purpose of recruitment and training in preparation for a general uprising that was vaguely mooted to coincide with the Commonwealth Prime Ministers' conference of September that year.

As with earlier incursions, this operation, although remarkably courageous, was extremely poorly planned and amateurishly executed and was doomed to failure more or less from the onset. Once inside Rhodesia, the two groups separated, each heading toward its own designated sector. This region of northwestern Rhodesia was extremely sparsely populated, and although wildlife was abundant, firearm discharges were obviously inadvisable, so shooting for the pot was impossible. A member of the Midlands group was sent ahead to purchase food, but he abandoned the group, leaving behind his weapons and equipment but taking with him most of the operational funds.

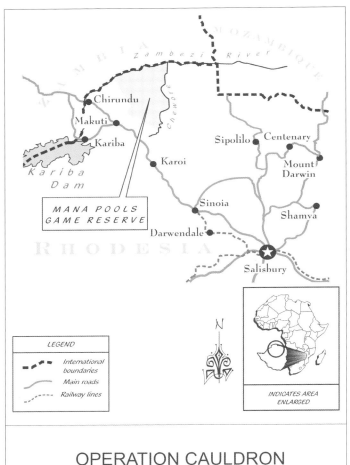

OPERATION CAULDRON

Source Genevieve Edwards

The group quickly disintegrated and the operation dissolved.

On 10 August 1966 the Nkai group was spotted by a geologist working for the Anglo-American Corporation who reported his suspicions to the local police at Binga, located on the western tail of Lake Kariba, from where a combined police and army operation, codenamed Grampus, very quickly swung into action.

All the members of the Nkai group were accounted for without a shot being fired, and Operation Grampus was officially terminated on 18 August 1966. What was interesting though, was something of a continuation of the ongoing hostility between police and army that had begin during Operation Pagoda. The operation was handled by a combined BSAP–RAR force that from the onset was characterized by a conspicuous lack of collaboration.

According to the most reliable account of Operation Grampus, contained in Alexandre Binda's history of the RAR, *Masodja*, the police remained detached and unwilling to cooperate, leaving 1RAR's Major David Heppenstall in a position where he had to garner intelligence that was not shared with him, and anticipate police mobilizations by keeping a close eye on them. "Every time we saw a police vehicle loaded up with armed men leaving the police station we would leap into our transport and roar after them…"[*] Some measure of revenge was achieved when on an

---

[*] Binda, Alexandre. *Masodja*, (30° South Publishers, Johannesburg, 2007) p. 205.

Operation Cauldron. Soldiers of the RAR played an integral role in this operation, working closely with the RLI. It was during this operation that the more experienced RAR soldiers came to accept the RLI as peers. *Source Masodja*

overnight patrol the RAR was able to demonstrate their operational superiority by having rations and basic survival equipment that were not shared with the police details who had none.

This was the basic pattern of events as 1966 gave way to 1967. Throughout 1967 and during the early months of 1968 hostile incursions into Rhodesia continued, growing in scope and expertise but not really achieving much in the way of tactical or strategic advantage. Through a combination of incisive intelligence-gathering and highly responsive military action, Rhodesian security forces mounted a series of operations codenamed Cauldron, Cosmic, Griffin, Mansion, Vermin. Nickel and Gravel that confronted both ZANU and ZAPU forces attempting to infiltrate into Rhodesia from Zambia, wherein they were ruthlessly run to ground and obliterated.

The two most notable operations within this cluster were Nickel and Cauldron, and these require brief examination.

By 1967, with the accelerated return of military cadres from training abroad, ZAPU began to feel more confident about the prospects of mounting incursions into Rhodesia on a larger and more organized scale. It was also at this time that ZAPU forged what would be a controversial alliance with the armed wing of the South African ANC, known as *Umkhonto we Sizwe*, or MK. At some point in mid-1967 ZAPU was approached by the ANC with a proposal for joint operations. The objective for MK was to establish a conduit of infiltration through northern and western Rhodesia for its trained members attempting to infiltrate South Africa. Military cooperation between South Africa and Botswana tended to preclude the movement of aggressive elements en route to South Africa through Botswana, leaving only this region of Rhodesia as a possible alternative. Other factors also made western Rhodesia an ideal transit route. The inhabitants of the region predominantly spoke Sindebele which, thanks to its root similarity to Zulu, meant that MK cadres could communicate and be understood over most of the region.

The root of the controversy was that this alliance appeared to make no sense to either the Pan Africanist Congress of South Africa or ZANU, both of which warned against offering any excuse to

The RLI's C/Sgt Wood with the MAG on fixed lines in ambush position in the Zambezi valley, 1968.

South Africa to deploy forces into Rhodesia. ZAPU functionaries and historians have maintained that this was a moot point, and that South Africa had already deployed significant force into the country, which is a rather unabashedly political interpretation of the facts, confirmed by southern African military historian Peter Stiff who was a serving officer with the British South Africa Police at the time, and who informed the author that he had no knowledge of any official South African armed deployment in Rhodesia. Stiff suggests that there may very well have been liaison personnel in the country, and perhaps individuals in a private capacity, but that would have been the limit of South African involvement at that point.

One of the most authoritative proponents of an earlier involvement of South African manpower in Rhodesia is Dumiso Dabengwa, ex-ZAPU intelligence supremo, and a voice not easily rejected. However, ZAPU came under such relentless and universal criticism for this alliance that motive to manipulate the facts certainly did exist, particularly criticism levelled at ZAPU by members of the OAU and Frontline States, observing that ZAPU had no business forging foreign alliances in the face of its inability to find common cause with ZANU.

Nonetheless the alliance, for better or worse, went ahead, and against this backdrop the first combined MK/ZAPU unit, numbering just under 200 men, crossed the Zambezi at the

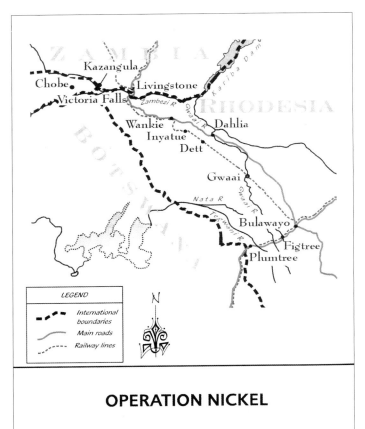

OPERATION NICKEL

Source Genevieve Edwards

Follow-up operations in the Zambezi valley during Operation Nickel.

A patrol commander checks his map while his men take a break in the heat of the Zambezi valley during the early days of Operation Nickel.

Gwaai Gorge situated between Victoria Falls and Kazungula. The presence of the group in the Wankie game reserve was reasonably quickly detected, with the first major engagement occurring on 13 August between the combined guerrillas and a Rhodesian force comprising units of the Rhodesian African Rifles and the Police Anti-Terrorist Unit (PATU).

During this operation, codenamed Nickel, the Rhodesians met with stiff resistance, neutralizing the guerrilla force only after several hours and with the intervention of Hunter strike jets deployed by the Royal Rhodesian Air Force. The operation concluded in September 1967 with the loss recorded of seven members of the Rhodesian security forces and some 30 guerrillas killed. This had been a significantly more challenging encounter than any hitherto, proving that the salad days of easy victory over untrained amateurs were at an end.

Needless to say, and after careful examination of accumulated intelligence, an offer of security assistance was indeed made to Rhodesia by South Africa through the Rhodesian Central Intelligence Organization, an offer which was quickly accepted. Soon thereafter a detachment of 2,000 South African Police members posing as riot police arrived in Rhodesia supported by much needed South African Air Force helicopters.

Meanwhile, between December and January 1968 a second large ZAPU–MK force numbering some 200 trained men crossed into Rhodesia from Zambia and established themselves in the Chewore controlled-hunting area in northern Rhodesia, east of Lake Kariba. For several months they moved backward and forward between Zambia and Rhodesia shuttling in supplies ferried across the Zambezi by inflatable watercraft. Constant contact was maintained with Lusaka through the use of high-frequency radio transmitters. Their temporary fortification was carefully hidden from aerial observation with a Viet Cong-style network of underground tunnels. However, they carved a wide footpath through the sandveld as they worked to ferry in large quantities of supplies. This alerted a patrolling National Parks game scout, David Scammell, who in turn alerted the authorities. Within a day the police and army were on the scene.

Operation Nickel. Two insurgents surrender to a combined RAR and RLI patrol. *Source Masodja*

Soon afterward a Joint Operations Centre (JOC) was established and on 15 March 1968, the Royal Rhodesian Air Force was placed on standby. Three days later contact was initiated in the Mana Pools area by a small RLI patrol, assisted by members of 1RAR, during which eleven out of a group of fourteen guerrillas were killed. One security force member also died.

The main camp was located during follow-up operations, forcing a request for air support as a security force patrol came under heavy fire from a group of some 60 well-armed guerrillas. In the meanwhile, the main body of the infiltrating force split up into smaller groups, some attempting to return to Zambia while others dispersed into the Sipolilo farming area. Ongoing follow-ups accounted for 58 members killed, 48 of whom were ZAPU and 15 were members of *Umkhonto we Sizwe*. Of the remaining force, 51 were captured and nine were thought to have returned to Zambia.

As the 1960s drew to a close, the two principal nationalist organizations were forced to step back and reflect on the fact that six years of military operations in Rhodesia had achieved absolutely nothing. Attempting to meet the combined might of the Rhodesian security forces in a head-on clash of arms was a simple recipe for suicide. Groups of revolutionary insurgents had displayed remarkable courage in their willingness to cross the Zambezi and march into the waiting arms of almost guaranteed annihilation, and while this might have served to build a respectable bedrock of revolutionary mythology, it was advancing the cause of liberation in Rhodesia not one iota.

As the 1970s dawned the exiled liberation movements withdrew

An RAR patrol in the Zambezi valley before the landmine became a menace. *Source Masodja*

their forces and ceased offensive operations in Rhodesia, after which they sat down to review and assess past performances. A complete overhaul of the current revolutionary war strategy was required, and it took some time for this to take place. In the meanwhile the northern border regions of Rhodesia, the Zambezi valley and hinterland, quietened down, and white Rhodesia was inclined to believe that the war had been won. Security vigilance was retained, of course, but between 1969 and 1971 very little was seen or heard of organized insurgent activity in the north of Rhodesia, and a sense began to prevail that all was well in Rhodesia.

Left: Operation Nickel. A wounded prisoner is brought in by helicopter.

Above: A guerrilla prisoner is handed over to Special Branch during Operation Nickel.

CHAPTER THREE:
THE POLITICS OF REBELLION

The Unilateral Declaration of Independence of November 1965 has been a decision debated by historians since the day it was made. There were two immediate ramifications. The first was that Rhodesia immediately became the subject of United Nations sanctions. These initially were slow to be rolled out, leading to the accusation that British prime minister Harold Wilson threw the book at Rhodesia, one page at a time. It is also true that the United Nations as an organization fulminated richly, but was also, on an individual membership basis, slow to put in place the measures that would make international sanctions most effective.

The second ramification, slower to mature, but probably in the long term much more impactful, was the fact that Rhodesia separated herself from 75 years of military integration with Britain in a single, surgical stroke. Winston Field, the first Rhodesian Front prime minister, who preceded the much more hawkish Ian Smith, made the point on the question of full independence from Britain under a minority-rule constitution, that it would immediately provoke a war. Maintaining imperial links with Britain, on the other hand, under terms that already very much resembled full independence, would mean that if the internal situation devolved into war then it would be a British war, fought by British troops with the ostensible weight of the British military establishment behind it.

The net result of Smith's decision to provoke a breach by an unconditional demand for independence under a minority rule was that Rhodesia then stood alone, confronting not only the full weight of world opinion, but also the combined resolve of black Africa in its determination to crush the rebellion. Under conditions of international sanctions, rendering arms procurement both difficult and expensive, Rhodesia would fight a war that was manifestly unwinnable, morally indefensible and anachronistic in terms of its stated objective to preserve white hegemony in Africa.

Backing up the tide of black liberation now threatening white Rhodesia, Mozambique, Angola and South Africa was the Soviet Union, Communist China, Cuba and almost every black African nation state. This allowed Ian Smith to smudge the lines of pure race ideology and claim that Rhodesia stood alone in defence of Western–Christian values in the face of a dark tide of communism sweeping southward through Africa.

This might have carried some weight with white Rhodesia, a sentiment echoed in fringe quarters of Britain, France, the United States and some Commonwealth countries, but it manifestly failed to impress any world government, and Rhodesia remained unrecognized as the 1960s drew to a close.

From 1965 through to 1980, the politics of post-UDI Rhodesia were characterized by an ongoing process of settlement talks in an effort to find a solution to the political impasse created by the rebellion. Initially these talks took place between the British and Rhodesian governments, effecting a continuum of the raw personal antipathy that existed between Rhodesian prime minister Ian Smith and British prime minister Harold Wilson.

The essential theme of discussion between the two parties was a return to legality, or how it would be that Britain could directly reassert control over Rhodesia in an effort to guide the process toward independence under very defined terms. These terms included the principle of unimpeded progress to majority rule,

HMS *Tiger* (launched 1945), in Portsmouth Harbour, Hampshire for Portsmouth Navy Day 1980.

Royal Navy assault landing ship HMS *Fearless* at Sinclair's Bay, Scotland, during the exercise Northern Wedding, on 10 September 1982.

guarantees against retrogressive amendment of the constitution, immediate improvement in the political status of blacks, progress toward the ending of racial discrimination, and the most vital point—that the British government be completely satisfied that proposals for independence had the support of a majority of the population and not the white-dominated electorate.*

This the British narrowed down to a formula that glorified in the acronym NIBMAR, or No Independence Before Majority Rule. This Smith countered with the now infamous comment made in a 1976 radio broadcast, stating: "Let me say it again. I don't believe in black majority rule ever in Rhodesia, not in a thousand years."

It therefore stands to reason that nothing of substance was achieved by these negotiations, although a distinctly imperial theme was struck when two rounds of talks were held respectively on board two Royal Navy vessels, HMS *Tiger* and HMS *Fearless* respectively, moored off the British enclave of Gibraltar. An interesting yet irrelevant feature of the HMS *Tiger* talks, held in December 1966, was the fact that Harold Wilson evidently chose this Churchillian setting to impress Smith with the grandeur and power at his disposal. Smith, however, a Royal Air Force combat veteran, was piped aboard with full ceremony, and toasted aboard ship in the officers' wardroom in a ceremony to which Wilson was not invited.

Two years later, in October 1968, the two met once again, this time on board the HMS *Fearless*, in a round of talks that concluded not only with an even less substantial result, but in an almost irreconcilable mood of acrimony between the two prime ministers. The mood of white Rhodesia remained one of fierce loyalty to the institutions of Britain, to the Crown and what remained of the empire, but with a deep loathing for the British government of the

day, of labour politics in general and of the creeping spinelessness that was perceived to be the modern character of Whitehall. This sentiment was enhanced immeasurably by the banning of any official Rhodesian delegation to the Cenotaph on Armistice Day, which cut so deeply into the Rhodesian sense of patriotism and of belonging to the British family that in many respects the involvement of any British individual or agency in the process of negotiating with Rhodesia marked an immediate recipe for failure. On 2 March 1970, Rhodesia severed all links with the Crown and declared herself a republic.

There was muted celebration, and a certain amount of sober introspection. Five years after UDI Rhodesia remained unrecognized by any country in the world. Most unnerving to those in the inner circles of security and government in Rhodesia was the fact that South Africa, on the surface an obvious ideological ally of white Rhodesia, did not present the united front in support of the rebel colony that most observers prior to the declaration of UDI would have expected. There were many reasons for this, some personality driven—Smith had a tendency to be abrasive and doctrinaire, frequently taking the position that 'you are either with me or against me', with very little appetite for the middle ground, and so invested in the utter moral correctness of his position that any criticism rankled so deeply it could not be tolerated. Other reasons were practical—the South Africans at that time were looking at a changing strategic map of Africa, and tending toward the idea that rapprochement, using the colossal weight of South African economic ballast as inducement to the cash-strapped nations of the north that would fall in line with the formation of an African commonwealth of sorts with South Africa as a senior partner.

This policy, known as détente, was the brainchild of South African prime minister John Vorster, and as quixotic as it might seem in retrospect, it nonetheless consumed South African foreign policy in regard to Africa for most of the early half of the 1970s, and certainly the roots of its conception can be traced to the late

---

* The bugbear throughout the Rhodesian standoff with the British was this differing concept of the popular will. The Rhodesian government clung to the legitimacy of a qualified electorate comprising mostly whites while the British demanded the full and unqualified representation of the general population.

British Labour Prime Minister Harold Wilson.

Ousted Portuguese Prime Minister Marcelo Caetano.

South African Prime Minister John Vorster.

Freimo's Joaquim Chissano. *Source Agência Brasil*

Mozambique regional & provincial

Source Kerrin Cocks

Mural depicting *Viva o 25 de Abril* (Long live the 25 April Revolution), Coruche, Portugal. *Source Júlio Reis*

was primarily against South Africa's hegemony over South West Africa (Namibia), which lies outside the scope of this narrative, but in Mozambique the threat to South Africa of a black, Marxist-orientated takeover was more directly economic. South Africa was very dependent on Mozambican migrant labour for the viability of the country's massive gold mines and, moreover, the Mozambican port of Lourenço Marques had in recent years become an essential overspill facility for South African imports and exports.

None of this was insurmountable, but a resolution to the issue without unnecessary unpleasantness appealed to South African prime minister John Vorster, and he felt that if the only sacrifice was white Rhodesia, which was manifestly doomed anyway, then it was worth trying.

Before the full implication of all of this was made directly known to the Rhodesian government, and Ian Smith in particular, events in Mozambique and Angola did indeed reach a tipping point, an event which probably had more to do with the domino effect of war in southern Africa that occurred from 1976 onward than anything else hitherto.

The wars in Mozambique and Anglo were both costly and politically unpopular at home. The fascist regime of Marcelo Caetano held fast to the idea that the retention of Portugal's

1960s as Rhodesia was finding her feet in this new reality.

A major impetus for the evolution of détente as South Africa's response to the *Swart Gevaar** was the increasingly inescapable fact that Portugal was losing her two main African colonial wars, Mozambique and Angola. This presented a number of potentially uncomfortable realities for South Africa. In Angola the threat

---

* Black Peril.

overseas provinces was a matter of national prestige. This sensibility, extremely impractical under the circumstances, bearing in mind Portugal's economic status in Europe, owes its origins to the 1884–5 Berlin conference, and the event known as the Scramble for Africa that followed. Portugal was the senior partner in African colonization, with Portuguese mariners being the first around the Cape of Good Hope in 1488, and the Portuguese the first European power to make landfall on the coast of East Africa. However, during the latter half of the nineteenth century, Portugal began to lose ground to the British, the Germans and the French, making a valiant effort to keep up appearances and, through the retention of her two key African possessions, maintaining the shreds of national prestige that economics and political influence alone could not justify.

This anachronistic ideal persisted into the 1970s, notwithstanding the strangulating effects of the war, a mood of rebellion in the military that made the effective prosecution of the war daily more difficult.

The strategic advance of Frelimo from it rear bases in Tanzania saw it very quickly assume effective control of all the northern provinces of Mozambique: Zambezia, Niassa, Cabo Delgado and Nampula—crossing the all important Zambezi river into Tete province in 1970. Tete had hitherto been a key defensive barrier for both the Portuguese and the Rhodesians.

Correspondingly the Portuguese prosecution of the war became increasingly apathetic and ineffective. Disaffection in the ranks of the Portuguese armed forces also began to assume alarming proportions. This trend continued until matters reached a head on 25 April 1974 when the right-wing government of Marcelo Caetano was ousted in a left-leaning military coup staged by the Armed Forces Movement, a committee of low-ranking Portuguese military officers opposed to the wars in Mozambique and Angola.

The Carnation Revolution, as the coup was styled, came as a complete surprise to the vast majority of white Rhodesians. There had been some awareness of a pending event in senior intelligence circles, but what was in effect a complete surrender by the Portuguese had not been anticipated. A 26 April communiqué issued by General António de Spínola, head of the hastily formed *Junta de Salvação Nacional*, effectively declared an end to the overseas campaigns. What this meant in practical terms was that notice had been served that Portugal would be handing over power in its two key territories of Mozambique and Angola to whoever was available to claim it.

In Angola this was the *Movimento Popular de Libertação de Angola* (MPLA), the first among equals of Angolan liberation movements, and in Mozambique the ubiquitous Frelimo. As white Rhodesia paused to ponder this, the blunt reality of a black, Marxist regime assuming power in neighbouring Mozambique began to come home. Frelimo could hardly be expected to be friendly to white Rhodesian interests, and so the likelihood was extremely high that at least one, but probably both of the main anti-Rhodesian liberation movements would be granted operational access to Mozambique. The net effect of this would be the opening up of a hostile front running 600 miles from the Zambezi river in the north to the Limpopo river in the south.

From that point things began to move quickly. An agreement was negotiated between Portuguese government officials and Frelimo that was signed into existence on 7 September 1974, allowing for a transitional government pending a formal takeover that was to be led in a caretaker capacity by Frelimo's Paris representative Joaquim Chissano. Independence from Portugal was achieved by Mozambique on 25 June 1975. Within six months war had effectively come to eastern Rhodesia.

The only hint of a silver lining visible on this extremely dark cloud was the sense among white Rhodesians that if South Africa had hitherto been coy about throwing her military weight behind the defence of Rhodesia, that this omen would change her mind. No such thing.

In July 1974, three months after the Portuguese coup, South African prime minister John Vorster met Ian Smith in Salisbury for talks.

CHAPTER FOUR:
A NEW PARADIGM

Military action is a method used to attain a political goal.
While military action and political affairs are not identical,
it is impossible to isolate one from the other
— Mao Zedong

The epiphany, when it was finally reached, was that a war of liberation in Rhodesia would, by necessity, be an asymmetric war, and could not therefore be won in conventional terms on a battlefield of the Rhodesian choosing. A more revolutionary tone of warfare would be required, which would in itself require a complete overhaul of the general military strategy of both organizations to include a comprehensive political element and a more general politicization of the masses.

A number of militants destined for the mid- and upper-command strata of both revolutionary movements were by the late 1960s receiving training in Red China where they were being introduced to the teachings of Mao Zedong and others on the matter of people's revolution, and the principles of guerrilla warfare. The essential philosophy of Mao in this regard can be defined most succinctly in his most famous quote on the matter:

The ZANLA Commando Group under training. Instructors in the front row are, from left: Cde Chibede, Cde Zitterson Zuluka, Cde Oliver Shiri and Cde Dragon Patiripakashata, all of which are *noms de guerre*. *Source Zimbabwean Ministry of Information*

"The guerrilla must move amongst the people as a fish swims in the sea." What is implied by this is that a war of popular liberation, fought against an incumbent and technically superior power, can only hope to be successful if it has popular support, and is pursed as a composite military–political struggle wherein the loyalty of the masses is achieved through education and politicization, leading to an eventual undermining of the regime, the occupation of territory and ultimately military defeat.

There was a broad-based and concurrent embrace of this concept in many quarters of the Zimbabwean liberation movement, with ZANU, and its military arm ZANLA, probably accepting the philosophical underpinnings of it more readily than ZAPU. ZAPU, and its military arm, ZIPRA, which found the bulk of its military support and ideological direction from the Soviet Union, tended to take a more conventional view of the war, formulating a strategy it called the Turning Point Strategy, which we will examine in a moment. For the time being, however, the evolving revolutionary strategy of ZANLA had a more immediate impact on the prosecution of the war.

Herbert Chitepo was quoted in an interview published in a Danish newspaper, as observing: "It is useless to engage in conventional warfare with well-equipped Rhodesian and South African troops along the Zambezi river."

This was a manifest truism, but a shrewder sense of the situation followed. Herbert Chitepo revealed in 1972 a complete reverse of hitherto accepted policy. From now on, he said, his party intended to reverse the errors of the past by politicizing and mobilizing the people before mounting any attacks against the regime. He went on to state that the object of any direct military action from then on would not be an attempt to defeat the Rhodesian security forces in battle, but to harass and attack vulnerable targets—the effect of which would be to force the Rhodesian Army to over-extend itself. In this way white manpower needs for defence would serve

to override the demands of commerce and industry, with the result that the country would eventually collapse. It was a simple strategy that had every chance of succeeding—particularly since the opening of the Tete front in Mozambique.

ZANU then began a two-pronged policy of withdrawing active units from the theatre and replacing them with reconnaissance groups and political commissars whose objectives were the education of the masses in the aims and objectives of the revolution, in preparation for a promised new phase of the war. Coupled with this, ZANU began wooing the Frelimo leadership, ostensibly the Castro-like Samora Machel, who now effectively controlled the Tete province and had it in his power to relieve the Zimbabwean liberation movement of the difficulty of crossing the Zambezi river in order to infiltrate Rhodesia. With the blessings of Frelimo, ZANU could establish rear bases in the liberated portions of Mozambique and have access to relatively easy avenues of infiltration into the northern quadrant of Rhodesia.[*]

In the meanwhile the education of the masses in the north of Rhodesia was rolled out with a chillingly Africanesqué regard for the finer points of violence. The method applied was very simply to illustrate the rewards of the revolution—the return of the land and political emancipation—coupled with a demonstration of the price of disloyalty, and this was usually achieved through the selection of one or more individuals in an assembly who were tortured and killed on the grounds of being sell-outs, thus conforming to the philosophy of Chinese tactician Sun Tzu: "Kill one man, terrorize a thousand."

---

[*] Samora Machel, along with all the other key regional leaders, and the OAU, still did not recognize the legitimacy of ZAPU, and offered access to Mozambique only to ZANU. ZAPU, however, was engaged in a deep internal crisis, and for the time being was unable to respond. So in the short term the excellent opportunities offered by the advance of the war in Mozambique were not available to the Rhodesian movement. This would change.

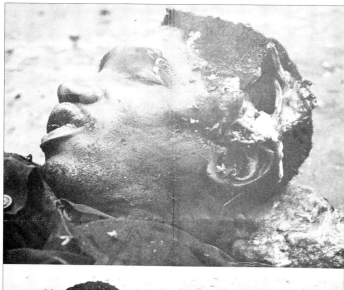

Mozambican President Samora Machel.

Tanzanian President Julius Nyerere.

"Kill one. Terrorize a thousand."
Source Rhodesian Ministry of Information

Rhodesian security forces worked with the Portuguese authorities in Mozambique to counter the guerrilla threat to Rhodesia as well as that of Frelimo's occupation of the northern Mozambican provinces.

The political ideology applied to this process was a combination of orthodox Marxist–communist principles, in keeping with the preference for both the language of the material masters of the revolution and a tendency at the time toward a synthesis of orthodox communism and African traditional communal values into an ideology-styled African socialism, largely the brainchild of Julius Nyerere, but to a greater or lesser extent adhered to by all the new generation of African leaders, and a call to local memory in the styling of the struggle as the Second Chimurenga.

The reference to an earlier struggle was a very shrewd political strategy, and was based on a number of separate facets. The first was the fact that the north of Rhodesia was the heartland of an ancient dynasty known as Mwene Mutapa, or Monomatapa, which recalled very much the glory days of the Chishona language group prior to the decline of empire and the arrival of the amaNdebele, and later the arrival of the white man. In addition a call to two powerful spirit mediums of the early occupation period, Kaguve and Mbuya Nehanda, offered the opportunity to apply a deeply symbolic spiritual context to the current struggle, which gave it tremendous social legitimacy that pure communism or Marxism could not have achieved in the minds of African peasants.

A related point in this regard is the fact that the local leadership structure had in many respects been usurped by the government. Traditional chiefs occupied a specific role within the local native administration, accepting official endorsement and official pay,

which effectively compromised them and rendered them irrelevant in the context of the current struggle. The beatification of long-dead spirit mediums, however, transferred the burden of traditional leadership away from the chiefs and into the realm of current mediums and local spiritual leaders. This branch of traditional leadership was so far uncompromised by official responsibility which offered the revolution a degree of ideological and social legitimacy that foreign concepts of proletarian advancement and collectivized economics could hardly have achieved.

From here a system of internal cells was devised that varied from place to place, but essentially involved localized revolutionary committees with appointed contact and liaison men and an organized system of reception, feeding, intelligence and succour. The effect of this programme was transformational. On the one hand youth flocked into Zambia and Mozambique to join the revolution, while on the other a collectivized sense of mission and commitment within the general population allowed for a renewed mobilization for war without a shred of intelligence reaching Special Branch through what had once been a highly tuned intelligence network of local informers. The ramifications of such disloyalty to the revolution had been illustrated to be terrible while a clearer understanding of the objectives of the revolution helped rally the masses to the cause.

OPERATIONS INTO TETE PROVINCE

Source Genevieve Edwards

Helicopter pick-up at Nyamasota airstrip prior to an attack on Segurança camp in southern Tete province.

Support Group troops await uplift at Nyamasota.

Support Group RLI personnel in a deserted ZANLA camp during Operation Sable.

To the Rhodesian security establishment the first hint of trouble came as a consequence of an external SAS operation into Mozambique conducted in March 1972 as part of a more general Rhodesian SAS and RLI involvement in northern Mozambique. Rhodesian reconnaissance and hunter–killer units were deployed into Mozambique from 1969 through the early 1970s in an effort to bolster Portuguese operations attempting to stem the advance of Frelimo and frustrate its strategy, once the Tete front had been opened in 1968, of breaching the Zambezi river. SAS teams were at different times active as far north in Mozambique as the borders of Tanzania, Malawi and Zambia.

Implicit in this was not only the fact that the Portuguese were losing their grip on the region, but that their military prestige would not allow them to acknowledge the fact, so these operations were styled combined operations, although the combined factor tended often to be cosmetic. Portuguese irregulars rarely engaged, and apart from much expenditure of ammunition, and a great deal of posturing, very little appetite for engagement existed.

A March 1972 attack on the Matimbe base in the Msengezi area of Mozambique yielded a haul of documents indicating very clearly that ZANLA elements had begun exploratory infiltrations alongside Frelimo units into the southern Tete province adjacent to the Rhodesian border, demonstrating that ZANU had indeed succeeded in its diplomatic efforts to secure acceptance by Frelimo, and had quite clearly arrived on the eastern border with Mozambique.

This was an extremely disturbing development. Rhodesian security forces were still groping blind in the face of a complete evaporation of all traditional intelligence sources, but the fact that the war was beginning to creep down the eastern border of Rhodesia was a source of enormous concern. In fact Prime Minister Ian Smith, usually very tight lipped on matters of security, broadcast a sobering address to the nation on 4 December 1972 that gave the first official hint that trouble was afoot: "The security situation is far more serious than it appears on the surface, and if the man in the street could have access to the security information which I and my colleagues in government have, then I think he would be a

ZANLA's Rex Nhongo.

ZIPRA's Dumiso Dabengwa.

Altena Farm, adjacent to the Chiweshe TTL in the Centerary farming area, was identified as the first target for the new phase of ZANLA's war.

ZANLA opened its summer campaign of 1972 with attacks on isolated white farms in the Centenary district. Landmines were used effectively by the guerrillas and caught the security forces unprepared.

lot more worried than he is today."

Almost at the moment Smith issued this statement, a party of twenty-one armed men slipped into Rhodesia from Mozambique and were immediately absorbed into the civilian population of the Chiweshe Tribal Trust Land. The group, led by a tough, motivated guerrilla leader by the name Rex Nhongo, was an advance party of ZANLA tasked with firing the first shots in this new phase in the war and to gauge thereafter the effectiveness of the Rhodesian military response.

After a short reconnaissance, the first target was identified as Altena Farm, a private agricultural property located in the Centenary farming area adjacent to the Chiweshe TTL. The property was subjected to a fairly superficial machine-gun and rifle attack before the group slipped back under cover to gauge both the effectiveness of their cover and the inevitable Rhodesian security response.

In the meanwhile, the property owner, Marc de Borchgrave, took refuge with his family on a neighbouring farm, Whistlefield, which was itself attacked a few days later.

The first Rhodesian casualty was RLI Corporal Norman Moore who was killed by a landmine blast during the Whistlefield follow-up. This was a an early manifestation of what would thereafter be a textbook ZANLA tactic. Hitting soft economic targets, seeding the area thereafter with anti-tank mines before fleeing back into the relative safety of surrounding Tribal Trust Lands. To this would be added the ubiquitous roadside ambush that became an increasingly deadly feature of civilian life in rural Rhodesia.

However, in the meanwhile, the first stage of the Rhodesian response was to establish Operation Hurricane, a JOC, which would be the first permanent operational area established in Rhodesia. In due course these would spread to encompass the entire country, but for the moment the main theatre of war remained the northern border region adjacent to the Zambezi valley, and here operations were focused as attempts were made to make sense of what had just happened.

Much of the failure of Rhodesian security policy was a failure to recognize the legitimacy of the struggle. Whether it was an authentic response, or simply verbiage for public consumption, the Rhodesian prime minister maintained the firm belief that

a majority of black Rhodesians supported both his government and the concept of minority rule in general, maintaining that the average black man in the street felt safer and more secure under competent white government than facing the prospect of black majority rule patterned on the emerging dictatorships and plutocracies emerging all over black Africa.

This was manifestly not the case. The urban unrest of the 1960s had been based on popular support, and after the aims and objectives of the revolution had been properly digested in the rural areas, black support for the struggle became almost universal. Rhodesian security forces suddenly found themselves chasing invisible terrorists. Intelligence dried up, no one knew

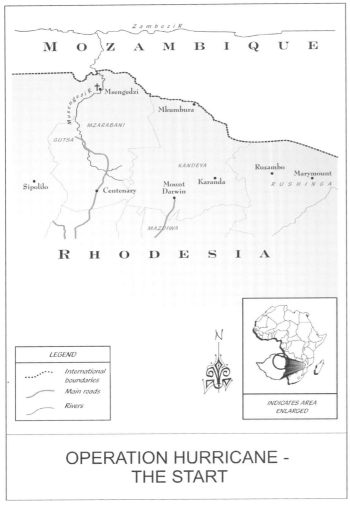

The RAR moves to sub-JOC Mtoko during Operation Hurricane. The main JOC for this operation was Mount Darwin. *Source Masodja*

Early days of Operation Hurricane: the 1RAR ops room in the Sipolilo camp. *Source Masodja*

OPERATION HURRICANE - THE START

Source Genevieve Edwards

Operation Hurricane: an Internal Affairs keep. These forts were manned by district administrators who monitored the local population. They were often soft targets for the guerrillas and frequently came under attack.

anything or had seen anything, and while punitive measures against local populations thought or perceived to be harbouring terrorists became commonplace, the fact remained that nothing the Rhodesian security forces were either willing or mandated to do could compare in terror value to the tactics of the guerrilla movements. So the wall of silence remained unbroken, and insecurity gradually began to spread over a wider area of northern Rhodesia. Farm attacks, landmine incidences and roadside ambushes were the preferred targets as Herbert Chitepo's strategy

of forcing the Rhodesian security forces to over-extend themselves in an effort to be at all places at all times.

In the meanwhile, the government augmented field security activity with a raft of new emergency regulations that empowered the authorities to impose collective fines, confiscate cattle and burn villages where community members were suspected of aiding and abetting terrorists. In addition the maximum term of imprisonment for supporting the insurgency was raised from five to twenty years alongside a mandatory death sentence or life imprisonment for terrorist activities. The sentence for recruiting terrorists was set at 20 years with an additional forfeiture of property.

Implicit in all of this was an admission that the authorities had lost the battle for the hearts and minds of the people. In recognition the government then adopted arguably its most controversial strategy of social containment of the entire war period, the introduction of protected villages. This was a concept borrowed from the British in their containment of the Malayan and Kenyan emergencies, and more recently the Portuguese in their efforts to limit the contagion liberation ideology among the masses.*

This in essence was a policy of rounding up the local population from large areas of the surrounding countryside and relocating them into large and fortified villages, allowing access in and out only under controlled conditions, thereby restricting guerrilla

---

★ The Portuguese version was known as *aldeamentos*.

access to the local populations in an effort to frustrate the ideology of the guerrilla being the fish and the population the ocean.

The concept was spun along the lines of protecting the population from the danger and pernicious influence of the guerrilla movements, but the reality was to prevent guerrilla groups finding easy support and succour within the rural countryside. It was a fairly transparent strategy, and was deeply unpopular among local blacks, but it was widely applied and in due course spread to operational sectors countrywide.

Militarily, the established strategies of cross-grain patrolling of the vulnerable border regions, coupled with traditionally excellent intelligence coverage, increasingly began to yield less of a tangible result. As the pivotal moment of truth drew closer—the epoch-changing 1974 military coup in Portugal—an increasing amount of official and unofficial thought began to be applied to new and creative strategies to wage an effective counter-insurgency war.

CHAPTER FIVE:
A NEW WORLD AND A NEW STRATEGY

The year 1976 opened with an immediate and massive escalation of the war. The Portuguese military coup had yielded a perfect storm of circumstances that pitched Rhodesia into what had become an unwinnable phase. A series of attacks was registered along the eastern border with Mozambique, a 600-kilometre frontier of rugged mountains and wide open sandveld, superbly accessible from forward bases in Mozambique, representing a ground-coverage conundrum that the Rhodesian security forces could quite obviously hope to contain.

How matters had come to this was quite simple. Robert Mugabe, incarcerated in Sikombela Detention Centre, emerged after a bitter internecine power struggle as the undisputed leader of ZANU. Detained since 1964, he was released from detention a decade later in December 1974, consequent to events associated with South Africa's détente policy, and also at a point coinciding with the ascension to power in Mozambique of Frelimo. Mugabe fled Rhodesia for Mozambique soon afterward, and there he established ZANLA as the dominant, in fact only Zimbabwean liberation movement operational in that country. This series of shrewd, but also extremely competent political manoeuvres, placed not only Mugabe himself, but his political party ZANU, in the dominating position in regard to the competition between the two main liberation factions to ultimately assume power in a free Zimbabwe.

Having acquired this commanding strategic position, Mugabe then set about building an army. He secured the support of Josiah Tongogara, the substantive commander of ZANLA, which was at that time headquartered in Tanzania, effectively transferring the onus of loyalty from Nadabaningi Sithole to himself. This then left the way open for him to seek material support from Red China, Romania and East Germany, among other Eastern Bloc powers, which was all very quickly directed toward the creation of a significant land army.

In parenthesis, it is worth noting that this rapid evolution of political cohesion and military preparedness tended in terms of strategic direction to echo the Maoist philosophy of the human wave. With lavish quantities of basic infantry equipment flooding into the ZANLA armoury, and a massive influx of recruits, the structure of ZANLA became one of a numerically copious force of nominally trained cadres superficially armed with AK-47 assault rifles, RPD light machine guns and RPG rocket launchers, supplemented by TM-46 anti-tank landmines and Model-24-style stick grenades.

Throughout 1976, ZANLA incursions spread rapidly throughout the Manicaland and Victoria provinces, which ZANLA had divided into a number of operational sectors. These were: *Takawira* Sector, *Chitepo* Sector, *Tangwena* Sector, *Monomatapa* Sector and *Musikavanhu* Sector. Below these, adjacent to the Gona re Zhou National Park, were three further sectors that were numbered and not named. This was because they were situated in tribally divergent areas where ZANLA commanders were reluctant to use chiShona names for fear of giving offence to local people.

The Rhodesian government covered the same area with two additional JOCs codenamed Thrasher and Repulse. The populous and agriculturally-rich eastern third of Rhodesia, hitherto largely unaffected, suddenly became the epicentre of the war.

The pattern of infiltration into Rhodesia was reasonably quickly identified. Most active ZANLA guerrillas entering Rhodesia, or poised to enter Rhodesia, had been trained in Tanzania.* These were shipped down the coast, disembarking either at Beira or Maputo, the newly renamed Mozambican capital. From Beira a majority was driven to a large rear base facility located on the Nyadzonya river not far from the provincial capital of Manica province, Chimoio. From there infiltration was primarily via the Honde valley and into the hinterland of Inyanga and the wider Eastern Highlands. Farther south, from Maputo, insurgents were either transported by rail or road up the Limpopo corridor, making use of Frelimo logistics and transport facilities to form up and orientate before deployment into Rhodesia.

All this was reasonably quickly established by Rhodesian intelligence. Implicit in this revised guerrilla strategy were efforts to once again hit soft targets and melt away into the local Tribal Trust Lands, which would, now that Rhodesian security forces were

---

* Senior personnel tended to be trained overseas. Low-level combatants received more localized training.

The charismatic Josiah Tongogara, ZANLA's substantive commander, headquartered in Tanzania.

facing enormously attenuated operational areas—effectively three quarters of the country encompassing the borders of Zambia, Mozambique and Botswana—stretch the available manpower resources of the country to breaking point. Quite clearly a new response was required, and it would not be very long before the Frontline States and the international community would be made aware of what this would be.

News broke on Tuesday 10 October 1976 of a pre-emptive raid that had taken place the day before in Mozambique. The Selous Scouts, Rhodesia's premier pseudo–infantry special force unit, had audaciously entered Mozambique in a heavily armed vehicle convoy, with troops and vehicles, disguised in Frelimo uniforms and livery, where they penetrated the ZANLA Nyadzonya base, then housing upward of 5,000 trained and semi-trained cadres, and in an hour or more of concentrated slaughter, killed some 1,200 members, and wounding several thousand more. The losses to the Rhodesian security forces as a consequence of this operation were zero.

The magnitude of this event took some time to digest, and it goes without saying that what was achieved in military terms was lost in what was unavoidably a public relations nightmare. From a tactical point of view, the operation was both brilliantly planned and brilliantly executed, but the graphic images that circulated worldwide in the aftermath, aided by the finely tuned ZANU propaganda machine, tended to eclipse that fact in favour of its portrayal as a Rhodesian-perpetrated massacre of civilians and refugees.

The fact that the camp had been largely unarmed, and that a number of non-combatant personnel had been caught up in the mayhem ought not in a clear analysis of the operation to obscure the fact that Nyadzonya was a legitimate military target. That casualty figures were so extraordinarily lopsided can be explained by the fact that the operation achieved its objective of total surprise, to the absolute professionalism of those responsible for the planning and execution of the raid, and, of course, to the notable difference in military competency of the two sides.

This, then, set the tone for the future conduct of the war. From that point onward the genie was out of the bottle. Rhodesian military attacks against neighbouring states then became a regular feature of war reportage. The strategy had the twin objectives of inhibiting the ability of guerrilla groups to orientate and mobilize in forward bases, mainly in Mozambique and Zambia, but also to discourage both countries from providing support and facilities within their sovereign territory for groups hostile to Rhodesia. The pummelling of Mozambican and Zambian transport and economic infrastructure was an intended corollary of Rhodesian

cross-border raids, and it certainly did impact the welcome of both liberation movements in their host countries, although the decision was never made to expel either, and nor to completely remove support for the liberation struggle.

Initially the main focus of attacks tended to be in Mozambique against ZANLA and Frelimo targets, in particular those located in the Manica province, and within an operational orbit of the provincial capital of Chimoio, but also those along the long Limpopo transport corridor that linked Maputo with the southern interior of Mozambique, leading to the Rhodesian border and the lonely and isolated southeast of the country. The Selous Scouts were regularly active here, and a number of large-scale, combined assaults utilizing the Selous Scouts, the RLI and SAS took place between 1976 and late 1979, the most significant of which will be dealt with later.

For the moment, however, this became increasingly the pattern of operations. From 1976 onward the country fell under a complete security blanket comprising operations Hurricane (northeast), Thrasher (east), Repulse (southeast), Tangent (west–southwest), Grapple (Midlands) and Salops (Salisbury). The understanding was, once Mozambique had opened as an active front, and once incursions from Botswana into Rhodesia became a more established fact of the war, that efforts to contain the situation within the country would largely be hopeless. This was the practical manifestation of Herbert Chitepo's strategy to cause the Rhodesian security machine to over extend itself and ultimately collapse.[*] Large areas of the country, in particular the more remote TTLs, were ceded to de facto guerrilla control, with the security force presence largely confined to fortified bases, and security force movement limited to heavily armed patrols or convoys. Most of the main agricultural areas became effective no-go areas, with agricultural operations either curtailed or severely limited, and efforts to remain on the land dependent on heavy security and achieved at severe personal risk to those willing to 'carry on'.

Thus the regular and special force units of the Rhodesian security forces—the SAS, the Selous Scouts and the RLI—to a large extent concerned themselves with taking the war to the guerrilla movements both in Mozambique and Zambia, keeping both movements on the back foot, and successfully inhibiting the large-scale incursions that might very well have brought the war to an end much earlier—while the territorial battalions, the irregulars and the national service independent companies were deployed largely in ground-coverage operations, patrol and garrison duties. The understanding now was that the war was militarily unwinnable, and the security role had become one of containment as a political solution to the crisis was sought.

★ Herbert Chitepo had by that stage been assassinated by a Rhodesian CIO agent in Lusaka. He was killed on 18 March 1975.

CHAPTER SIX:
THE POLITICS OF SURVIVAL

In June 1970, British Labour prime minister Harold Wilson was defeated by Conservative Edward Heath, introducing a season of tentative hope in Rhodesia that some sort of accommodation on the vex question of independence could be reached. Heath, however, had no interest in muddying his term of office with an irresolvable question like Rhodesia, so he handed the matter over to his Foreign Secretary, Sir Alec Douglas Home, and old friend and supporter of white Rhodesia.

Here at last was a man with whom Rhodesian prime minister Ian Smith felt that he could deal, and the decade opened with a renewed sense of optimism on both sides of the Rhodesia question. Indeed, cordial meetings and talks began almost immediately, proceeding smoothly through the remainder of 1970 and 1971, resulting in an agreement between the two governments that was announced in mid-November 1971.

Rhodesian demands had been broadly acceded to, NIBMAR had been slimmed down to a simple promise of political parity while black political progress would be protected by little more than Rhodesian guarantees. In order to establish the broad-based acceptability of these proposals it was agreed by both sides that a British commission of inquiry, chaired by a former Lord of Appeal, Lord Edward Holroyd Pearce, would be sent to Rhodesia to take evidence on the matter.

It is interesting here that Rhodesian prime minister Ian Smith agreed to this provision. The Rhodesian electorate had been narrowly defined under the 1961 constitution by a conditional education, property and taxation status that tended to limit black inclusion to a very few landed and wealthy blacks. Nonetheless, Smith, based on information that he tended to filter through the somewhat unreliable Department of Internal Affairs, ignoring more reliable intelligence supplied by the CIO, appeared to believe with complete sincerity that his government enjoyed wide grassroots support in Rhodesia.

In fact so confident was Smith of an endorsement of his government by the black majority that he authorized the release of a handful of detained nationalists representing both movements in order that a moderate internal black political front could be formed to impress upon the Pearce Commission not only the impartiality of the Rhodesian government, but also the sagacity of the current agreement. This gambit failed. The African National Council (ANC), under the leadership of local Methodist bishop Abel Muzorewa, so successfully organized massive grassroots opposition to the terms of the 1971 settlement that Lord Pearce was forced to return to Britain and report to the House of Commons that the implementation of the agreement was impossible.

Zambian President Kenneth Kaunda.

Smith and the Rhodesian government were stunned by this reverse, and while publically it was claimed, not altogether untruthfully, that the delays in the arrival of the Pearce Commission had given the opportunity to more aggressive nationalist elements to intimidate the wider black population, the fact remained that the last reasonable chance of a settlement had slipped through the fingers of the Rhodesian government. By then the pendulum of nationalist advantage was on the return swing, and never again would

US Secretary of State Henry Kissinger.

Prime Minister Edward Heath.

Sir Alec Douglas Home.

Methodist Bishop Abel Muzorewa.

Jason Moyo.

terms as advantageous as those offered to Rhodesia on board the HMS *Fearless* and *Tiger* be on the table.

Smith had painted himself into a corner. He had led the white Rhodesian public along a road of confrontation with the British that in the 1960s had seemed to favour Rhodesia, but by the 1970s, with the proliferation of black rule throughout Africa, the militancy of the United Nations and the Commonwealth, and global public opinion that neither favoured nor supported any sympathetic accommodation with white Rhodesia, the moment had quite clearly passed. If minority rule in this small, landlocked country had once seemed reasonable, it was now a clear anachronism that had no place in the modern world. And what is more, there were few in Rhodesia, white or black, who were still blind to the writing on the wall.

The British then more or less washed their hands of Rhodesia. The terms of the 1971 settlement remained on the table, but British diplomacy made itself available only to endorse whatever agreement was reached internally by Rhodesians themselves. Noteworthy is the fact that when this position was assumed the vast majority of the substantive black nationalist leadership in Rhodesia was incarcerated and beyond the reach either of arbitration or the public expression of any opinion. There was no chance in the short term that any kind of meaningful negotiation could take place, let alone an agreement being reached. And there the matter for the time being resided.

In the short term there was still a sense within Rhodesia that the war could be settled on the battlefield. There were some within the white community voicing dissent, but very few, and on the whole the electorate remained firmly behind Prime Minister Ian Smith and his right-wing caucus. The war went on, and in fact Rhodesian optimism was buoyed somewhat by news filtering through from Zambia that the two nationalist movements had imploded into a bout of fratricidal infighting that did nothing so much as serve the interests of white Rhodesia.

The dynamics of what has since become known in Zimbabwean liberation mythology as *The Struggle Within the Struggle* are both complicated and very simple. In perhaps the simplest possible terms, the saga began with a decision by ZAPU chairman in exile, James Chikerema, to in 1970 personally conduct a British film crew on a tour of an insurgent rear base located in Zambia where large numbers of ZIPRA cadres were preparing for deployment into Rhodesia. The exiled executive erupted in disbelief when the news of this became general. Rhodesian intelligence was recognized as being exceptionally finely tuned and vigilant, and offering them visual reference to the next wave of insurgents to enter Rhodesia seemed like an act of negligence at best, and of criminal stupidity at worst.

Chikerema was a poorly educated trench fighter of the revolution, and actually had no place at the higher echelons of party leadership. He was reputed to have been appointed deputy to Joshua Nkomo solely because he lacked either the intelligence or the gumption to ever mount a challenge for the leadership. Having then assumed leadership in exile upon Nkomo's detention,

he found himself understudied by a number of much more gifted men. The most notable among these was Jason Moyo, who would emerge later as a more rational head of the party in exile.

The minutia of this internal contradiction are not really relevant here, other than to say that a series of public thrusts and parries were enacted, out of which Chikerema emerged the more wounded. He then left the leadership of ZAPU to Jason Moyo, leading the tatters of his own faction to ZANU, then reasonably united as an organization and focused on the prosecution of the armed struggle. To a sector of the ZANU leadership, Chikerema proposed the formation of a unity movement, which had in fact been something that the OAU and the Frontline States had been urging on all parties to the Rhodesian struggle for some time.

This call for unity succeeded in attracting a handful of key ZANU leaders, not by any means a majority, but enough among them to pitch ZANU into an internal contradiction that quickly and severely undermined its ability to function. Out of this emerged a third movement—the Front for the Liberation of Zimbabwe (FROLIZI)—which was formally launched on 1 October 1971, at coincidentally more or less the same time that the centrists of both parties were uniting within Rhodesia to form the African National Council (ANC).

The formation of FROLIZI, notwithstanding the fact that it fractured the combined movement even further, and undermined the ability of all three Zimbabwean liberation movements to achieve anything meaningful on the battlefield, was well received by the OAU and the Frontline States, which forced a certain amount of rapprochement between the old and new leadership of ZAPU, and some reluctant acceptance of FROLIZI on the part of ZANU.

In general though, the entire episode was a disaster for the prosecution of the struggle. In March 1973 a joint military command was formed in terms of an agreement brokered by the OAU that obliged all three liberation movements to declare their loyalty to a single command structure. All three swore to this, but the organ never functioned, and in the end matters returned essentially to a status where FROLIZI and ZAPU did very little in practical terms, with ZANU continuing to fight the war essentially alone.

By late 1972 the more considered predictions of the liberation leaders were proved to be correct. FROLIZI became a victim of its own irrelevance, and so did Chikerema. In due course the ZANU deserters rejoined the party on the understanding that none could hold an elected office for two years and Chikerema went looking for a home among the internal Rhodesian moderates. By 1974 FROLIZI was effectively dead and ZANU was once again the first among equals.

This was not the end of the affair. The internal contradictions underway in Lusaka, and the emphasis that had tended recently to be placed on the political direction of both parties, had the effect of diverting attention away from the military units and detachments languishing in the bush waiting for some definitive military direction. This presented an opening for Rhodesian intelligence, ever alert for an opportunity to stir the pot of conflict within the revolution—a pot that was never far from the boil anyway.

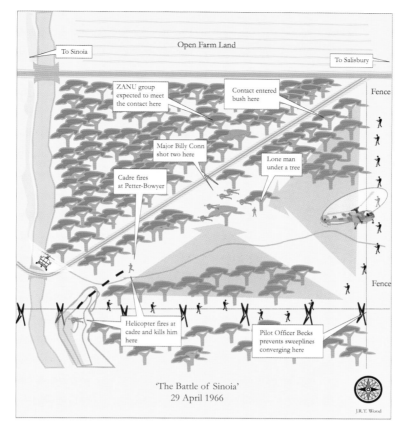

'The Battle of Sinoia'
29 April 1966

J.R.T. Wood

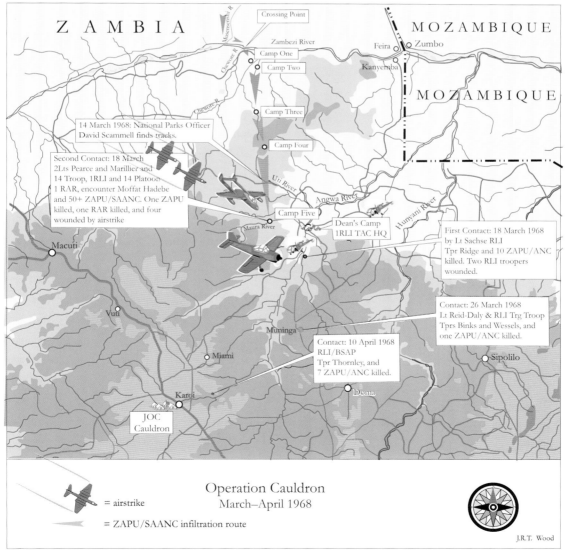

Operation Cauldron
March–April 1968

= airstrike

= ZAPU/SAANC infiltration route

J.R.T. Wood

RLI, National Parks and BSAP personnel display captured Russian weaponry, Zambezi valley, 1966.

Operation Hurricane
1972-1980

WLL = Wild Life Land
PL = Purchase Land
TTL = Tribal Trust Land
= Rhodesian Operational Areas

FAF9 = Forward Airfield
Flyde = Rhodesian Air Force Base

0   50   100   150   200   250
Kilometres

J.R.T. Wood

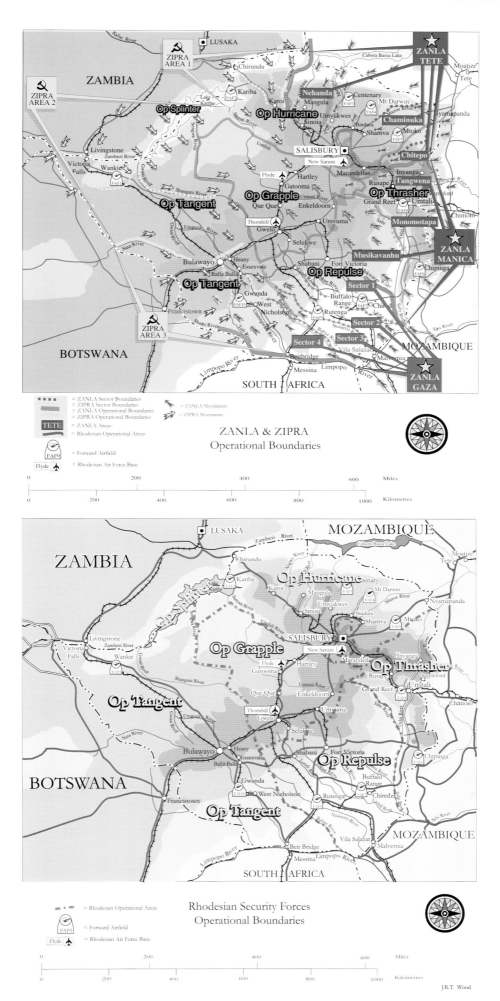

ZANLA & ZIPRA
Operational Boundaries

= ZANLA Sector Boundaries
= ZIPRA Sector Boundaries
= ZANLA Operational Boundaries
= ZIPRA Operational Boundaries
= ZANLA Areas
= Rhodesian Operational Areas

TETE

FAF9 = Forward Airfield
Flyde = Rhodesian Air Force Base

= ZANLA Movements
= ZIPRA Movements

Rhodesian Security Forces
Operational Boundaries

= Rhodesian Operational Areas
FAF9 = Forward Airfield
Flyde = Rhodesian Air Force Base

J.R.T. Wood

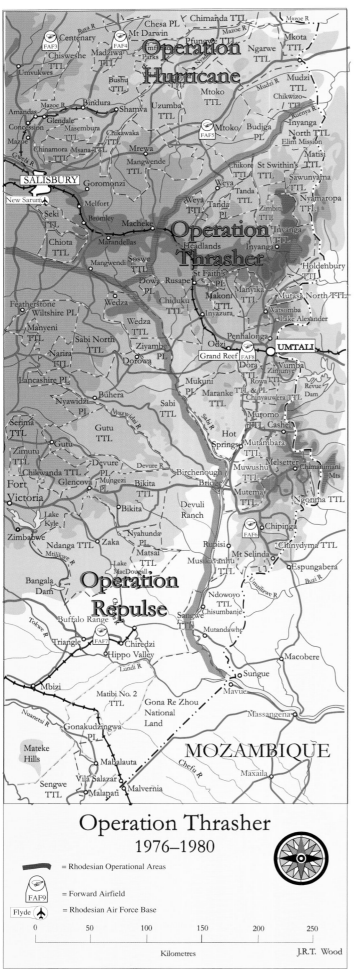

Operation Thrasher
1976–1980

- = Rhodesian Operational Areas
- FAF9 = Forward Airfield
- Flyde = Rhodesian Air Force Base

0   50   100   150   200   250

Kilometres

J.R.T. Wood

Hawker Hunter strike jets were pivotal in neutralizing the stiff resistance from the guerrilla forces during Operation Nickel.

Canberra bombers were used effectively during Operation Cauldron.

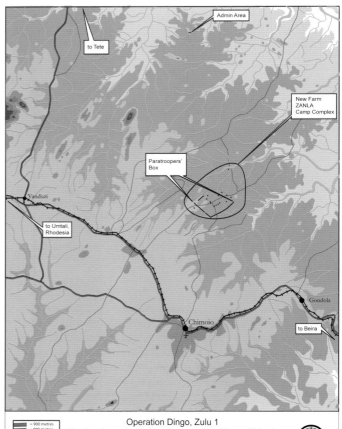

Operation Dingo, Zulu 1
The Attack on the ZANLA Camp at New Farm, Chimoio
Wednesday, 23 November 1977

0   5   10   15   20

kilometres

J.R.T. Wood

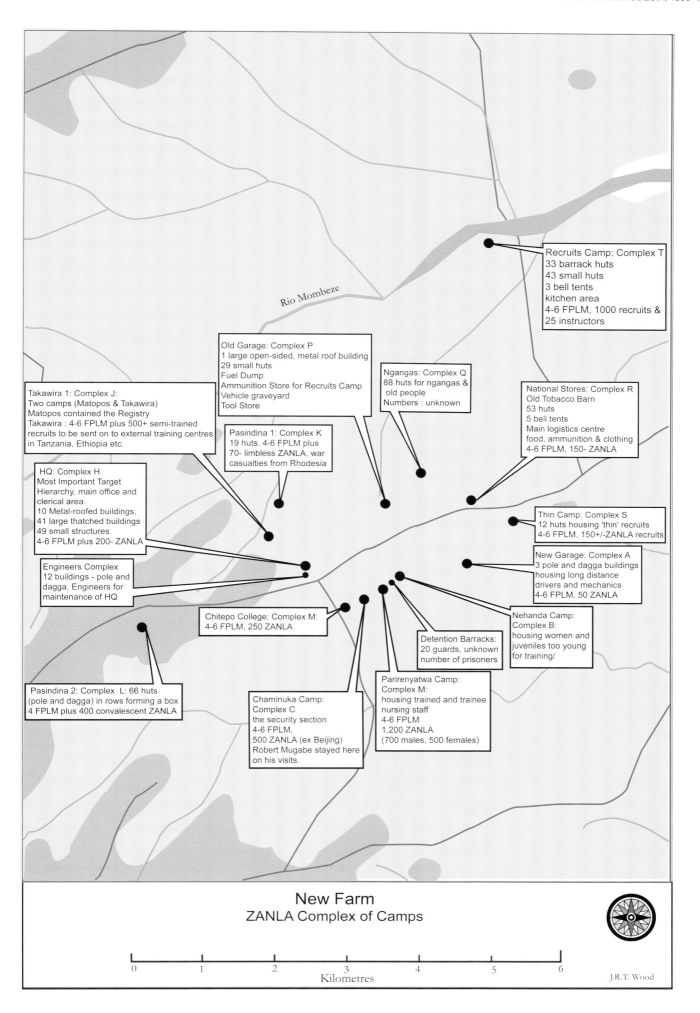

Rio Mombeze

Recruits Camp: Complex T
33 barrack huts
43 small huts
3 bell tents
kitchen area
4-6 FPLM, 1000 recruits &
25 instructors

Old Garage: Complex P
1 large open-sided, metal roof building
29 small huts
Fuel Dump
Ammunition Store for Recruits Camp
Vehicle graveyard
Tool Store

Ngangas: Complex Q
88 huts for ngangas &
old people
Numbers : unknown

National Stores: Complex R
Old Tobacco Barn
53 huts
5 bell tents
Main logistics centre
food, ammunition & clothing
4-6 FPLM, 150- ZANLA

Takawira 1: Complex J:
Two camps (Matopos & Takawira)
Matopos contained the Registry
Takawira : 4-6 FPLM plus 500+ semi-trained
recruits to be sent on to external training centres
in Tanzania, Ethiopia etc.

Pasindina 1: Complex K
19 huts. 4-6 FPLM plus
70- limbless ZANLA, war
casualties from Rhodesia

HQ: Complex H
Most Important Target
Hierarchy, main office and
clerical area.
10 Metal-roofed buildings,
41 large thatched buildings
49 small structures
4-6 FPLM plus 200- ZANLA

Thin Camp: Complex S
12 huts housing 'thin' recruits
4-6 FPLM, 150+/-ZANLA recruits

New Garage: Complex A
3 pole and dagga buildings
housing long distance
drivers and mechanics
4-6 FPLM, 50 ZANLA

Engineers Complex
12 buildings - pole and
dagga. Engineers for
maintenance of HQ

Chitepo College: Complex M:
4-6 FPLM, 250 ZANLA

Nehanda Camp:
Complex B:
housing women and
juveniles too young
for training/

Detention Barracks:
20 guards, unknown
number of prisoners

Pasindina 2: Complex L: 66 huts
(pole and dagga) in rows forming a box
4 FPLM plus 400 convalescent ZANLA

Chaminuka Camp:
Complex C
the security section
4-6 FPLM,
500 ZANLA (ex Beijing)
Robert Mugabe stayed here
on his visits.

Parirenyatwa Camp:
Complex M:
housing trained and trainee
nursing staff
4-6 FPLM
1,200 ZANLA
(700 males, 500 females)

New Farm
ZANLA Complex of Camps

0   1   2   3   4   5   6
Kilometres

J.R.T. Wood

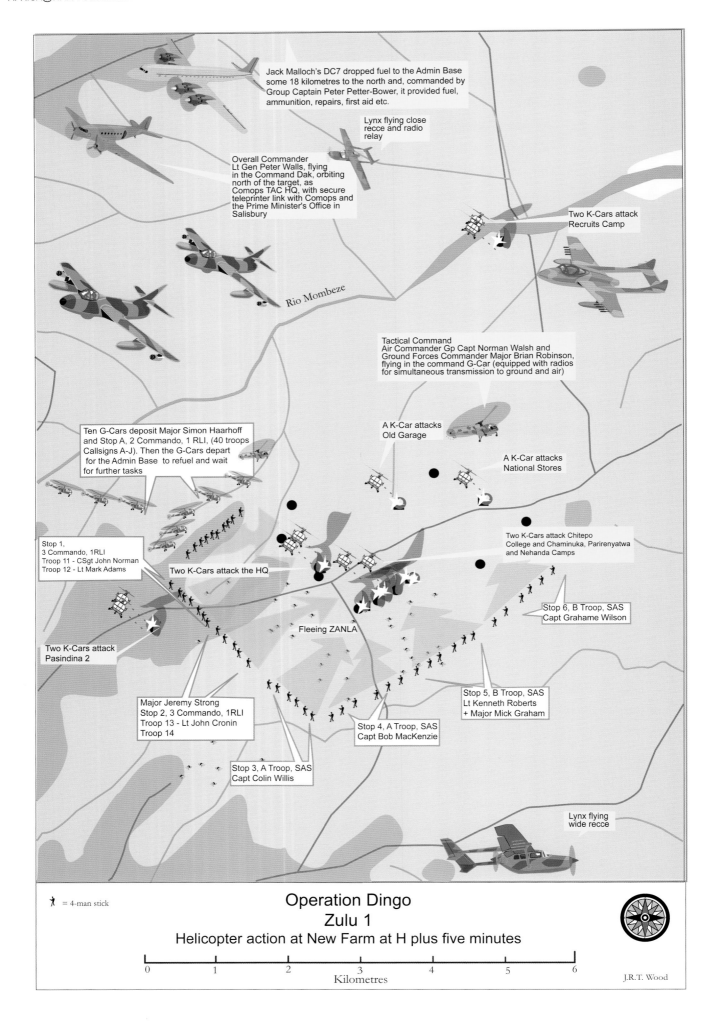

Jack Malloch's DC7 dropped fuel to the Admin Base some 18 kilometres to the north and, commanded by Group Captain Peter Petter-Bower, it provided fuel, ammunition, repairs, first aid etc.

Lynx flying close recce and radio relay

Overall Commander Lt Gen Peter Walls, flying in the Command Dak, orbiting north of the target, as Comops TAC HQ, with secure teleprinter link with Comops and the Prime Minister's Office in Salisbury

Two K-Cars attack Recruits Camp

Rio Mombeze

Tactical Command Air Commander Gp Capt Norman Walsh and Ground Forces Commander Major Brian Robinson, flying in the command G-Car (equipped with radios for simultaneous transmission to ground and air)

A K-Car attacks Old Garage

A K-Car attacks National Stores

Ten G-Cars deposit Major Simon Haarhoff and Stop A, 2 Commando, 1 RLI, (40 troops Callsigns A-J). Then the G-Cars depart for the Admin Base to refuel and wait for further tasks

Two K-Cars attack Chitepo College and Chaminuka, Parirenyatwa and Nehanda Camps

Stop 1, 3 Commando, 1RLI Troop 11 - CSgt John Norman Troop 12 - Lt Mark Adams

Two K-Cars attack the HQ

Stop 6, B Troop, SAS Capt Grahame Wilson

Fleeing ZANLA

Two K-Cars attack Pasindina 2

Stop 5, B Troop, SAS Lt Kenneth Roberts + Major Mick Graham

Major Jeremy Strong Stop 2, 3 Commando, 1RLI Troop 13 - Lt John Cronin Troop 14

Stop 4, A Troop, SAS Capt Bob MacKenzie

Stop 3, A Troop, SAS Capt Colin Willis

Lynx flying wide recce

$\dagger$ = 4-man stick

Operation Dingo
Zulu 1
Helicopter action at New Farm at H plus five minutes

0   1   2   3   4   5   6
Kilometres

J.R.T. Wood

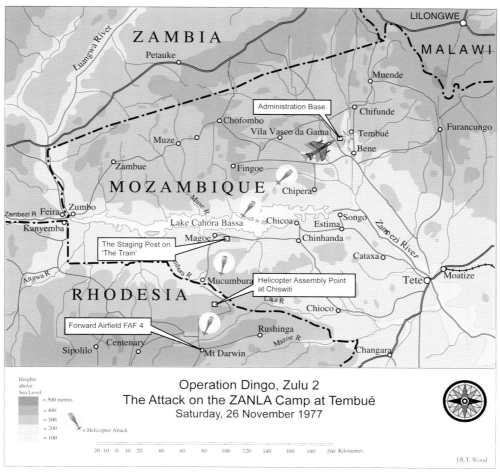

Administration Base

The Staging Post on 'The Train'

Helicopter Assembly Point at Chiswiti

Forward Airfield FAF 4

Heights above Sea Level
= 500 metres
= 400
= 300
= 200
= 100

= Helicopter Attack

Operation Dingo, Zulu 2
The Attack on the ZANLA Camp at Tembué
Saturday, 26 November 1977

20 10 0 10 20   40   60   80   100   120   140   160   180   200 Kilometres

J.R.T. Wood

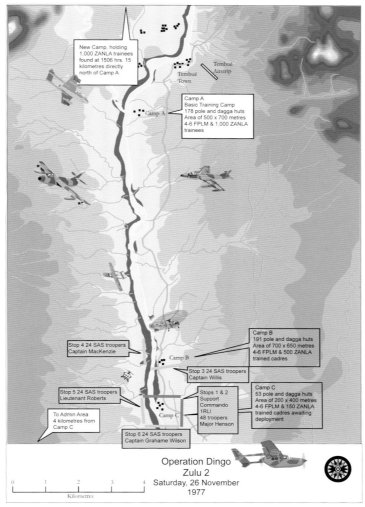

New Camp, holding 1,000 ZANLA trainees found at 1506 hrs. 15 kilometres directly north of Camp A

Tembué Town

Tembué Airstrip

Camp A
Basic Training Camp
178 pole and dagga huts
Area of 500 x 700 metres
4-6 FPLM & 1,000 ZANLA trainees

Stop 4 24 SAS troopers
Captain MacKenzie

Camp B
191 pole and dagga huts
Area of 700 x 650 metres
4-6 FPLM & 500 ZANLA trained cadres

Stop 3 24 SAS troopers
Captain Willis

Stop 5 24 SAS troopers
Lieutenant Roberts

Stops 1 & 2
Support Commando
1RLI
48 troopers
Major Henson

Camp C
53 pole and dagga huts
Area of 200 x 400 metres
4-6 FPLM & 150 ZANLA trained cadres awaiting deployment

To Admin Area
4 kilometres from Camp C

Stop 6 24 SAS troopers
Captain Grahame Wilson

Operation Dingo
Zulu 2
Saturday, 26 November 1977

0   1   2   3   4
Kilometres

A PATU stick, Centenary East, 1975.

RLI troops on the move again to hide from the Zambian air threat during Operation Cheese, 1979. *Source Ross Parker*

Above: Operation Cheese proved conclusively that the RLI could operate behind enemy lines as well as the SAS. *Source Ross Parker*

Left: SAS freefall into Zambia for Operation Cheese, 1979. *Source Craig Fourie*

In September, and again in November 1974, Special Branch made contact with various ZANLA sectoral commanders operating within the Tete province, and from a certain guerrilla commander known as Thomas Nhari, Special Branch members learned a great deal. It was established that separate power struggles were underway in Sikombela prison between ZANU treasurer Robert Mugabe and its leader Ndabaningi Sithole, and in Lusaka between exiled leader Herbert Chitepo and senior guerrilla commander Josiah Tongogara.

The mood in the field was dark. It was increasingly perceived that the political leadership in Lusaka had sold out to champagne lifestyles in the city while the fighting men had been left to languish in the bush. Chitepo, it is worth remembering, drove an old VW Beetle as his official vehicle, while Robert Mugabe was striving in Sikombela prison to rebuild the momentum of the struggle, none of which alludes to any personal aggrandizement or corruption, but such was the view on the ground, and needless to say Special Branch confirmed all the worst fears of the combatants and encouraged them to march on Lusaka and effect a coup.

This attempt at warfare by other means succeeded spectacularly, and what unfolded thereafter has since become known as the Nhari Rebellion. In November 1974 a large group of ZANLA combatants, headed by Nhari, made for Lusaka and attempted to oust the military leadership of the party. ZANU at that point was in flux anyway thanks to the ongoing power struggle between Mugabe and Sithole, coupled with a sense at the higher political levels of the party that negotiations germane to the détente process would produce a settlement, in which case military affairs were no longer particularly relevant.

The rebellion was left to ZANLA commander Josiah Tongogara to deal with, which he did from under a cloud of deep distrust for the political leadership. Thus the whole affair very quickly devolved into an internecine squabble, followed by a further devolution into a veritable fistfight involving every faction within the party, and creating new factions as a deadly and disproportionately bloody civil war was fought within ZANU.[*]

This episode enraged the Zambian president, Kenneth Kaunda, who had by then had about as much as he could tolerate of the unending disunity of the Zimbabwean liberation movements. The general insecurity created by the large number of armed factions on Zambian soil, none answering to any official chain of command, was a source of concern, as was the indiscipline displayed every time there was a disagreement within one or other of the parties. All this was inflamed by the mischievous activities of Rhodesian intelligence elements who were ubiquitous throughout the crisis.

At a few minutes after 08h00 on 18 March 1975, four months after the launch of the Nhari Rebellion, the morning calm of the Chilenje South suburb of Lusaka was shattered by an explosion that completely destroyed Herbert Chitepo's car, killing him and his bodyguard outright, but also the child of a next-door neighbour who was hit by a flying wheel. The act was perpetrated by a CIO assassin, Alan 'Taffy' Brice, an ex-British SAS operative who had been in the pay of the CIO for some time, and had been wreaking havoc in the Zambian capital—playing one feuding faction off against another.

This assassination was another spectacularly successful coup on the part of the Rhodesian CIO. Lashing out blindly, Kaunda, who had no idea who was responsible, and nor did he really care, ordered the mass arrest of ranking ZANU and ZANLA members, including Tongorara. He closed down the ZANU offices in Lusaka and convened a commission of inquiry to establish who was responsible for Chitepo's assassination.

The commission began its work in July 1975. A year later, ten days before the first anniversary of the murder, the report of the commission was signed and presented to Kaunda. The findings pointed the finger squarely at members of the ZANU Dare Chimurenga and the ZANLA high command. Josiah Tongogara was explicitly named, along with four other people. The underlying logic was presumably that Tongogara had ordered the hit to better align himself for the ultimate leadership of a free Zimbabwe.

Ultimately more than 1,300 ZANLA personnel ended up in Zambian prisons as a consequence of the affair, bringing military operations to a complete halt. Robert Mugabe issued a statement pointing the finger at Kaunda himself as the most likely sponsor of Chitepo's assassination, sparking an antipathy between the two men that would never quite heal, and also making plain his decision to remove his party from any negotiations with the Rhodesian government as part of the détente process.

Mugabe was not, in practical terms, the leader of ZANU yet, since Sithole remained to be formally deposed, but that would simply be a matter of time and procedure, at which point Mugabe would in every respect be the most powerful individual in the entire stable of competing nationalists.

In the meanwhile, as Robert Mugabe blamed the Zambians, and the Zambians blamed ZANU, in private there remained a strong suspicions that somehow the Rhodesians had been at the root of the entire episode, as indeed they had.

Back in Salisbury 1974 was the defining year of the South African détente policy. The mid-1974 meeting held in Salisbury between Ian Smith and his South African counterpart offered John Vorster the opportunity to finally lay bare to an incredulous and dismayed Ian Smith the fact that South Africa did not see a military solution to the Rhodesian crisis. Far from weighing in after the Portuguese coup with a massive infusion of military force, as most white Rhodesians had both hoped and expected, the South Africans seemed prepared to sacrifice Rhodesia for the sake of rapprochement with the militant and militantly plutocratic regimes that were by then well established across the sub-Saharan region.

In the short term Smith came under pressure to release the detained nationalists, to which, late in 1974, he acceded. The two principal nationalist leaders—Robert Mugabe and Joshua

---

* Thomas Nhari, incidentally, was executed soon afterward as Tongogara fought to regain control.

Nkomo—immediately returned to active engagement in the struggle, as Smith had morbidly predicted they would. John Vorster, meanwhile, set about cementing his relationship with Kenneth Kaunda, by organizing an all-party conference to be held in Victoria Falls. This was ostensibly to bring the leadership of white and black Rhodesia together, but in many ways it was staged for no better reason than to give Vorster an opportunity to meet with and woo Kenneth Kaunda into his stable of compliant African leaders.*

The Victoria Falls conference of 25 August 1975 was arguably the most ridiculous episode of a farcical chapter in the history of southern Africa. The Rhodesians were shackled by their dependence on South Africa for military shipments and the movement of Rhodesian rail traffic, and so complied with South African pressure to attend, while the various nationalists, dependent on their regional sponsors and the OAU, did likewise, and thus this crowning achievement of détente was staged with a crushing lack of commitment on the part of either side.

No mutually acceptable venue could be found, so the parties met in three South African Railways' train carriages parked midway between Zambia and Rhodesia on the Victoria Falls bridge. All the principal nationalists attended with the exception of Robert Mugabe—ZANU was represented by the largely impotent Ndabaningi Sithole—which in every respect confirmed the irrelevance of the conference. The combined nationalists, now flying yet another set of improvised unity colours styled the United African National Council (UANC), and led by the no-less-impotent Bishop Muzorewa, had merged temporarily under pressure from the OAU, and indeed for the most part were only attending because of pressure from the OAU and the Zambian government.

The conference failed, no agreement was reached, and in fact so indifferent were the Rhodesians to the affair that the Rhodesian delegation, led by Ian Smith, did not even bother to reconvene after lunch. It is notable that Ian Smith, in his memoir, *The Great Betrayal*, reflects rather ruefully on the fact that he returned to the venue after lunch at the Victoria Falls Hotel just to make sure that no members of the nationalist delegation were waiting, only to find the refreshments carriage that had been lavishly stocked by the South Africans with wine, beer and liquor to be completely obliterated, and not a nationalist was in sight.

The Victoria Falls conference was the last visible sign of détente, thereafter the Rhodesians returned to a war footing with the facts of the Portuguese coup rapidly unfurling. On 25 June 1975, Mozambique was granted independence, and all of the potential ramifications that this implied were multiplied by the unpalatable fact that all jailed nationalists were now free to exploit the situation.

Robert Mugabe wasted no time in slipping out of Rhodesia and making his way to Mozambique. He recognized that Mozambique would be the key to the next phase of the struggle, and in the midst of the internal contradictions wracking both ZAPU and ZANU, and notwithstanding the fact that he had yet to be recognized as party leader either within the party itself, or in any of the relevant African forums, he was determined to restart the struggle from here.

His first problem was to gain the acceptance of Samora Machel, the new president of independent Mozambique, who was less than delighted to discover the news of his uninvited guest. Ndabaningi Sithole still held the leadership of ZANU, coupled with the fact that ZANU had still not gained the acceptance of either the OAU liberation committee or the Frontline States. Mugabe was held in protective custody in Quelimane until some sense could be made of the tangled mess of Zimbabwean liberation politics.

The key to slicing the Gordian Knot came with a decision by a surviving core of ZANLA officers based at Mgagao Camp in Tanzania to issue an appeal to the OAU Liberation Committee for recognition, arms and funds while at the same time dismissing a generation of weak and ineffectual leadership with a blanket declaration of loyalty to Robert Mugabe. This resolution, known as the Mgagao Declaration, in one defining movement projected Robert Mugabe into the position of party leader, forced the reluctant forums and presidents of the continent to finally recognize ZANU and gave ZANLA a home in Mozambique. It also finally gave the party the focused and dynamic leadership that it had lacked. ZANU was now finally able to regroup, reform, train and arm to begin this new phase of the war with total and absolute commitment.

However, recognition of ZANU by the OAU didn't immediately take place after the Mgagao Declaration, leaving Mugabe again temporarily frustrated by the strict adherence to procedure that so characterized the organization. The OAU was still determined to see the UANC as the umbrella group under which all the liberation movements would agree to function, and so, in order to facilitate the flow of arms, another empty military formation was defined in order to represent the movement as a whole—the Zimbabwe People's Army, or ZIPA, which existed briefly, but in name only.

This meant that ZANLA once again found itself at the bottom of the list for the distribution of Soviet military support, forcing Mugabe to re-examine ZANU's external support network. This took him in new directions in search of arms and financial backing. He forged relations with Red China, Romania and Yugoslavia, sourcing arms, money and training. In due course four of the Frontline leaders paid him a visit in Quelimane and formally conceded that détente had failed, with each agreeing that there was now no alternative to total war. Mugabe was in business.

For South Africa, détente died upon the altar of her own military adventurism. Liberation in Mozambique was one thing—power had been handed over relatively cleanly to a single, principal organization, Frelimo—but in Angola three dominant organizations were vying for power. These were the MPLA, a Soviet-aligned revolutionary party, UNITA, a more western-aligned surrogate of South Africa, and the FNLA, also more western aligned, but supported too by Zaire, and fairly flexible in

---

* Félix Houphouët-Boigny of Côte d'Ivoire, William Richard Tolbert Jr. of Liberia, Léopold Sédar Senghor of Senegal and Mobuto Sese Seko of Zaire were some among those sympathetic to Vorster's overtures.

In the early stages of the Angolan campaign, the South African army soon realized they were outgunned. Equipped with G-2 5.5-inch guns, their artillery was vastly inferior to the MPLA's. Being an outdated Second World War design, the guns didn't have the range compared to the MPLA rocket launchers supplied by the Soviets. Operation Savannah was the last time they would be used by the SADF in conventional warfare.
Source Cameron Blake

its general ideology. UNITA and the MPLA dominated, with the MPLA being the better placed of the two, and since the Portuguese were basically willing to hand over power to whoever was available to receive it, the seeds of one of Africa's longest and most bloody civil wars was sown.

In support of the MPLA, the Soviets began to appear in Luanda in disturbing numbers, followed by even more significant numbers of Cuban advisers, each accompanied by large shipments of arms and all the other accoutrements of a major war. South Africa, herself under pressure over her ongoing less than legal occupation of South West Africa (Namibia), and actively containing an insurgency that was spreading across her common northern border with Angola, began to grow increasingly agitated at the growing Soviet and Cuban presence in Angola. Through support for UNITA, and a general willingness to take the fight to the enemy, South Africa stood poised for involvement in something far larger than a modest little war in Rhodesia.

The catalyst for this was US concern for Soviet Cold War proliferation in southern Africa, but with her recent defeat in Vietnam, Washington was extremely reluctant to engage militarily in Africa. Instead, the United States unleashed on the continent the power of US Secretary of State Henry Kissinger in a search for some sort of a proxy solution, and this they found in South Africa.

Dealing with South Africa on any level tended to result in bad publicity in black Africa, so Kissinger was naturally very cautious in his approach. In August 1975, however, South Africa—with covert CIA assistance and mute encouragement from the White House—launched an invasion of Angola, codenamed Operation Savannah. The objective of Operation Savannah was to influence events in Anglo, advancing in a month to within artillery range of the Angolan capital, and turning back thanks only to political jitters and a victory of Cuban brinkmanship. This effectively handed Angola over to the MPLA, realizing both Washington's and South Africa's worst fears.

These events ramified on Rhodesia thanks to the emergence of US participation in Operation Savannah, and the outcry heard across Africa at US support for and involvement with South Africa. Kissinger was then forced to look around for a foil, and it was on Rhodesia that his eyes fell.

Kissinger put a proposition to Pretoria that, under the circumstances, John Vorster could hardly refuse. He promised that American support for anti-Marxist forces in Angola would continue, and that no political pressure would be applied in the short term over the future of South West Africa. In addition, the United States would strive to overcome international resistance to the granting of $460 million in IMF credits to South Africa. In exchange for this South Africa had only to ratchet up the pressure on Rhodesia.

In September 1975, Ian Smith travelled to Pretoria for a meeting with Vorster and Kissinger. During this meeting Kissinger and Vorster played good cop bad cop with the unfortunate Rhodesian prime minister. Kissinger informed him first that a settlement with the black nationalists would need to take place sooner rather than later, and that failure to achieve this in the current US electoral term would leave the Rhodesians farther down the road dealing with Jimmy Carter. Vorster then added his quotient by informing Smith that unlimited South African support in the furtherance of war in Rhodesia was impractical. It was proving to be a drain on South Africa resources and a diplomatic burden in the wake of the Soweto riots of 16 June 1976.

Smith was assured, as he digested all these unpalatable facts, that both Mozambique and Zambia were desperate for a settlement, and would hold the nationalists' collective feet to the fire in order to ensure that a practical diplomatic solution could be found.

All this Smith doubted, but the fact remained that without South African support the war in Rhodesia would be lost, so he had no choice but to agree. Thus, as the war entered its most violent and decisive phase, the political leadership of Rhodesia was once again forced to tow the line in yet another round of what was perceived as fruitless political interference.

CHAPTER SEVEN:
THE RHODESIAN WAY OF WAR

The Rhodesian armed forces were relatively simply configured. It was a small army, some even compared it to the Israeli Defence Forces as the most deadly and battle-ready army in the world at the time, although most in Rhodesia felt that this was an unfair comparison. The Rhodesians, they thought, were far better.

By 1976, a point at which Rhodesia was undoubtedly at war, the machinery of war was arguably at its most effective. Operation Eland, the raid on the ZANLA Nyadzonya camp, was the first real indication of what the armed forces of the country were capable of achieving. There had been a time when the member states of the Organization of African Unity had mooted the idea of an African force to take on Rhodesia in order to forcefully settle the matter of UDI. In the rear of the forum Hastings Banda, elderly leader of Malawi, was heard to chuckle. Ten Rhodesian mercenaries, he told his colleagues, could whip five thousand African soldiers. If Smith commanded it, he added, the Rhodesian army could conquer the whole of east and central Africa in a week.

This was probably not entirely true, but certainly taking on the Rhodesians would cost a nation much in blood and treasure, and in the end there was none prepared to try it. Even the British recognized that attempting to regain control of Rhodesia by force of arms was not feasible. An armed and belligerent Rhodesia, bearing in mind the experience of two world wars, was something to be feared.

Operation Eland also introduced the Selous Scouts to the world. Humanitarians howled loud at the disgraceful slaughter that had taken place in Nyadzonya on that day, but military men, and military students, rather more quietly admired the extraordinary military prowess and daring that had allowed this to happen.

The Selous Scouts was one of two special force fighting units in the Rhodesian Army. The senior of the two, the SAS, or the *Supers*, was an elitist unit configured very much along the lines of the British SAS, which the Rhodesian SAS in fact was allied to in an honorary context as C Squadron (Rhodesia) SAS. It was elitist in the sense that it did not accept membership from blacks, which tended to limit its scope of operation to scenarios that did not require any merging or reconnaissance in highly populated tribal areas. It was deployed in standard special force operations, often in combination with the RLI, which by 1976 had been retrained as a commando unit, acting as a strike force in cross-border raids and in sabotage and surgical-insertion operations.

The Selous Scouts, on the other hand, was formed specifically with the purpose of infiltrating active guerrilla groups in a pseudo context, which required not only the recruitment of black servicemen, but also the induction of turned guerrillas as well as white handling personnel acculturated to a very high degree in native languages and social practices.

The unit evolved as a consequence of the merger of many

Malawian President Hastings Banda.

US Democratic President Jimmy Carter.

Aerial photograph, taken from a Canberra bomber piloted by Wing Commander Randy Durandt, of a muster parade at the Nyadzonya/ Pungwe base before the raid. A count revealed over 800 guerrillas on parade.

independent thought processes, each dwelling on the same basic conundrum. Allan Savory, an oft mentioned pioneer of military tracking as a Rhodesian security force discipline, was also a man on the visionary fringe of the military establishment, which was quite often a very lonely posting. From that vantage he propounded the fairly self-evident need for a more incisive style of warfare. This was a popular position in most quarters, but he also quite freely made known his political views—principally that the war was unwinnable, and that an urgent and inclusive political solution needed to be found sooner rather than later.

Despite those and other seditious utterances, Savory's ideas and practices had a lasting effect on the methodology of the Rhodesian war. The development of a dedicated tracking wing to the army answered one need of the war—rapid follow-up and quick closure. However, a handful of younger visionaries were also at work on an advancement on this concept.

In the Operation Hurricane area, Special Branch had long been hard at work developing a deeply rooted network of contact men and informants, overlapping on occasions into Mozambique. A parallel development underway involved pseudo-operational tactics using a handful of highly acculturated whites controlling a mixture of black police or army volunteers and authentic turned guerrillas.

Both threads of the same idea merged, and in due course small teams of pseudo operatives under the tactical control of one or more white handlers, and comprising mainly turned guerrillas, became operational under administrative control of the army, and adopting a name left vacant by an earlier armoured car regiment, the Selous Scouts.

The Selous Scouts became effective during 1973, coalescing into a formal regiment toward the end of that year, and immediately registering significant successes in penetrating guerrilla units operational in Rhodesia. These were either milked for intelligence, or an aerial assault was called in to take them out, quite often both. Tactical methods tended to be very fluid, but in essence these involved the covert deployment into an area of a pseudo group comprising ideally two white NCOs or junior officers and up to fourteen black operatives posing as an active guerrilla unit. The former would establishment themselves in a rear base and monitor and control the black members as they attempted to manoeuvre into a position of trust. The rear base was usually an OP located on high ground from where as much as possible of the surrounding countryside was visible.

The objective was, in the first instance, to gain the trust of local contact men and cell leaders in order to gain information on the whereabouts of genuine groups. Once trust was established, introductions would usually be made, after which the pseudo group would retire and an aerial assault would be called in.

In its first few months of operation the Selous Scouts performed magnificently. Affected guerrilla units were taken completely by surprise. In due course an appreciation of what was afoot was gained, and active guerrilla units began to counteract Selous Scouts' success with an elaborate system of protocols and code that levelled things out considerably. However, the signature weakness of guerrilla operations was a lack of effective radio communications between groups, and between active units and rear bases. Therefore any wider strategy needed to be rigidly planned, lacking fluidity should sudden change be necessary, because units had to be informed by runner and by the transfer of written orders. Consequently much written material was in circulation, and intelligence hauls tended to be very detailed thanks to this.

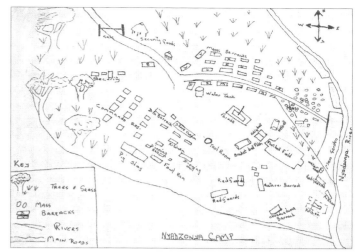

A ZANLA map of the base captured during the raid.

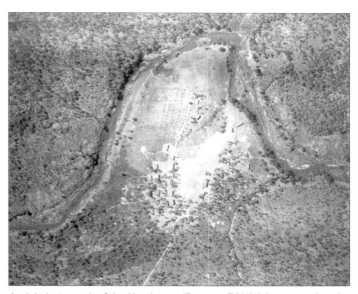

Aerial photograph of the Nyadzonya/Pungwe ZANLA base on a bend in the Nyadzonya river, Mozambique.

A close-up of the image above. An aerial photograph after the raid shows hundreds of guerrilla corpses (which can be seen with a magnifying glass).

Operation Eland, the raid on the Nyadzonya camp introduced the Selous Scouts to the world, dramatically and controversially.

Three Alouette III G-Cars on standby at a rural airfield.

A G-Car with a stick of four men and its door-mounted machine guns, .303 twin Brownings.

Key to the success of the Selous Scouts' pseudo strategy was a rapid deployment, vertical envelopment tactic known as Fire Force. Fire Force was used to devastating effect in combination with both Selous Scouts pseudo operations as well as the more orthodox territorial ground coverage operations.

Fire Force, as it was most commonly deployed, comprised a standby force of three Alouette III helicopters, or G-Cars, armed with door-mounted machine guns and configured primarily for troop deployment and support. Each helicopter carried four fully armed troops, the standard Rhodesian squad configuration, known as a stick. These were typically RLI, but the RAR was commonly deployed on Fire Force duty, as were occasionally the RR and independent companies. The latter tended to be the exception rather that the rule, however, and the RLI developed much of its reputation through its dominance and mastery of Fire Force.

Included in the air armada would typically be a fourth Alouette III, known as a K-Car, which would usually be armed with a formidable mounted 20mm cannon. A K-Car as a rule had room for only the pilot, the gunner-tech and the Fire Force commander. From 1977 onward an additional complement of 16 to 20 paratroopers could be deployed by a C-47 Dakota transporter. Highly effective air support was usually also available from one of the Rhodesian Air Force's multi-functional Cessna 'Lynx' aircraft, backed up by a squadron of Hawker Hunters should all this still not finish to the job.

A Fire Force would be located at one of a number forward airfields (FAFs) covering each of the operational areas. Selous Scouts typically operated in 'frozen areas' where routine security force activity had been suspended in order to avoid overlap and instances of friendly fire. Once a report had been received at a JOC, either from a Selous Scouts' call sign, or as a consequence of any other identification of a concentration of active guerrillas, the air force (RhAF) would be appraised and a Fire Force placed on immediate standby. In the instance of a decision to scramble a detailed briefing would be delivered before the formation took to the air. When the aircraft reached ten minutes from the target area, ground units would begin to verbally guide the command car on target by radio.

Once on target the command helicopter would propel steeply upward from treetop level to a height of 250 metres, or 800 feet above ground, which was the height at which the 20mm canon was typically calibrated. The G-Cars, in the meanwhile, would effect a rapid anti-clockwise rotation of the contact area in order

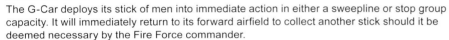

The G-Car deploys its stick of men into immediate action in either a sweepline or stop group capacity. It will immediately return to its forward airfield to collect another stick should it be deemed necessary by the Fire Force commander.

The deadly K-Car 20mm cannon.

to hedge in the enemy using concentrated door-mounted machine gun fire. The Fire Force commander would then quickly take stock of the situation before deploying troops. In the meanwhile, a Cessna Lynx, circling the contact area at a height of about 1,000 metres, would remain on the scene ready to engage the target with SNEB rockets, golf bombs or frantan, a locally produced napalm.

Troops would be deployed in stop groups to engage guerrillas attempting to flee ahead of sweeplines or an air assault. Paratroopers would also be available as a standby if reinforcements were required. If it was a large target the attack would be preceded by a 'softening up' by Hunter strike jets or Canberra bombers.

The principle of Fire Force became the tactical hallmark of the Rhodesian war, proving to be so successful that only restrictions on equipment, manpower and air assets limited the reach and effectiveness of this deadly tool. Toward the end of the war it was not uncommon for Fire Force units to respond to up to three actions a day, and on more than one occasion the entire complement of owned and borrowed air assets would take to the skies in massive versions of Fire Force visited against static installations and large guerrilla staging camps both in Mozambique and Zambia.[*]

The Rhodesia Light Infantry occupies a unique place in modern military mythology. There are many reasons for this, not least among them the fact that the RLI was a highly trained and lightly configured commando unit perfectly constituted to meet the demands of the theatre.

The unit performed brilliantly during the war, maintaining a nimble mobility and a hard-hitting aggression throughout the conflict that rendered this small, battle-hardened unit almost invincible on its own ground.

The RLI was formed in 1961 as a response to both the preponderance of black regular military battalions and the large numbers of blacks active within the local constabulary. It was felt that in the instance of a rebellion, a loyal and dependable white regular battalion would be essential. The recruitment net tended to be thrown fairly wide, and a number of South Africans and colonials signed up initially, but over the years many foreign nationals would serve in the ranks of the unit.[†]

Initially the RLI functioned as a light infantry, but it was reformed as a commando battalion in 1965. The reputation of the unit was forged largely through its work with Fire Force. A great component of the RLI myth is that of the minimalist *troopie*, clad in shorts, *takkies* and a T-shirt, plunging into battle several times a day with breathtaking daring and resilience. This defined the Rhodesian self-image, and in many ways defined the conduct of the war. The *Saints* were the iron fist of the Rhodesian Army. Any group of guerrillas who happened to look skyward to see a Dakota disgorging paratroops, or hear the low thump of an approaching helicopter, would know without a doubt that hellfire was coming.

The signal that called in that hellfire very often came as a consequence of exhaustive ground coverage operations routinely undertaken by the Rhodesia Regiment and the independent companies. Rhodesia Regiment battalions were associated with specific regions, with the principal battalions being based in Salisbury, Bulawayo, Umtali and Gwelo. The RR was almost exclusively territorial, although toward the end of the war regulars were to be found in the ranks of the regiment.

The independent companies, six in total, with a seventh formed briefly to accommodate a contingent of French volunteers, lay under the administrative control of the Rhodesia Regiment,

---

[*] South African helicopters, pilots and crew were on almost permanent loan to Rhodesia, although with varying degrees of commitment. As political expedience dictated, or at least permitted, Rhodesia fought most of her major cross-border actions with at least some connivance from the South Africans.

[†] The Rhodesian security forces did not make use of mercenaries in the truer sense. Foreign nationals entering service with the Rhodesian Army did so on the same terms of service as every soldier.

As Fire Force developed, 16 to 20 paratroopers would be deployed into the contact area.

Freefall paratroops deploy from a C-47 Dakota.

The Hawker Hunter combined grace with aggression.

The Canberra bomber.

The .303 Browning machine guns mounted above the main plane of the Lynx was a successful Rhodesian Air Force design and implementation.

but were independently commanded. This was an unorthodox arrangement, because within a typical British military formation, a company is controlled by a battalion headquarters while an independent company reports directly to brigade headquarters. The company is effectively independent, and is assigned to its own operational area.

The Rhodesia Regiment comprised eight battalions, numbering one to ten, with the 3rd and 7th (Northern) Rhodesia Regiment battalions having been removed after the break-up of the Central African Federation. The first major action fought by the regiment was the East Africa Campaign of the First World War. This proved to be a rugged and brutal deployment that claimed more lives through disease and exhaustion than combat, and eventually the regiment was removed from the line because of its inability to replenish manpower.

The Rhodesia Regiment was an orthodox irregular infantry formation sustained almost entirely by local territorial commitments. These varied over the years, growing in frequency and length as insecurity spread and as whites began to leave the country in ever-greater numbers. An average call-up lasted for six weeks. Men would assemble, usually in company strength, at a local drill hall to equip and brief. This would be followed by a two-day reorientation battle camp to zero in weapons and prime up for active service. From there the company would deploy within the country, usually within the prescribed area of the battalion, and in most instances attached to an established military camp, a forward airfield or a local farm or estate homestead.

A typical territorial operation would involve patrol, ambush and observation. A few territorial members found their way into the Selous Scouts and the SAS, but for the most part the Rhodesia Regiment was where the irregulars did their service. Initially, during the early phases of the war, a call-up was an opportunity for men to get out into the bush with the lads, spiced with

A Rhodesian observation post. *Source John Wynne Hopkins*

National servicemen of the Rhodesia Regiment's independent companies.

An RAR soldier and a Rhodesia Regiment machine gunner on patrol in the Zambezi valley.

justenoughdanger to make it fun. But as insecurity spread during the latter half of the 1970s, reaching a point in the last few years of the war that the entire country was a war zone, territorial call-ups became longer, more frequent and grimly concentrated as men were ever more thinly spread, and the demands of each day significantly more rigorous and dangerous.

The regiment was exclusively white for most of its existence, but again, during the latter years and months of the war, numbers of African Soldiers (AS), some regular, others territorial, found their way into RR companies. Likewise, toward the end of the war the independent companies fell under the administrative control of the Rhodesian African Rifles, at which point numbers of young blacks were recruited and conscripted.

This phenomenon, in part, was driven by a need for inclusion and rapprochement between the races, but also because the departure of whites from the country had been accelerating steadily since mid-decade, such that by 1979 almost an infantry company a month was disappearing from the country. There simply were not enough white personnel available to sustain the race exclusivity of the traditional white battalions.

The independent companies were the home of young school leavers and national servicemen disposing of their two-year-service commitment before being assigned to a Rhodesia Regiment battalion. Recruits were drafted directly from school, and usually national service was completed before university or apprenticeship. Intakes were given basic training at Llewellin Barracks located outside Bulawayo before being assigned to an independent company. Bases and barracks were in Wankie, Victoria Falls, Inyanga, Umtali and Kariba, and independent company troops basically performed a ground-coverage and garrison role. A young troopie might expect to man an observation post for dreary weeks, patrol endlessly on foot and in vehicles or spend interminable nights in an ambush position. The independent companies were usually commanded by a regular army officer, drawn most frequently from the RLI, assisted by regular senior officers and NCOs. Junior officers were quite frequently teenagers, and certainly all the junior NCOs were effectively schoolboys. The independent companies, however, provided a vital bulwark against the weight of guerrilla incursions into the country, and increasingly as the war progressed they entered full combat space, performing in many instances at least as well as the regular commandos of the RLI.

Operating much more informally, quite often as a sort of localized civil defence, was the BSAP Reserve, or Police Reserve. These were usually older men performing garrison duty, convoy escort, urban patrolling and homestead security. The BSAP itself adapted very quickly to the demands of internal insecurity and became at its core increasingly paramilitary. The BSAP Support Unit, as its name implies, functioned in support of the civil authority. Known as the *Black Boots*, Support Unit, comprising no more that forty white personnel, mainly officers, and some three hundred black personnel, operated as an armed field force in a counter-insurgency role.

An early photograph of PATU operatives, taken in September 1966, before the issue of camouflage and when FNs were in short supply. Reg Seekings, the driving force behind the PATU training regime, is on the far right.

Inspector Alan Stock (crouching), Patrol Officer Alan Murray, Constable David and Section Officer Dave Lawson on PATU duties at Karanda in the northeast, 1973.

PATU, or the Police Anti-Terrorist Unit, was formed in 1966 and made use of the skills and local knowledge of landowners and local residents in order to form responsive rapid-reaction teams to locate and deal with political or guerrilla activity on a local level. Most members of PATU would have had some military training, most would simply by exposure be both extremely versatile within the local communities and sensitive to any changes or disturbance. PATU was very active throughout Rhodesia during the war, and was regarded as a Police Reserve and civil defence commitment more than a routine call-up or draft.

The Rhodesian African Rifles was the oldest and most august of the Rhodesian regular battalions. There remained a sniff about it of the old colonial regiment, harking back to the days of the King's African Rifles and the German *Schutztruppe*. In those days native troops and junior NCOs served under the command of an elite corps of colonial officers whose exclusivity was premised on their fluency in language and in their sensitivity to the peculiar needs of the native.

Such was the case to a greater or lesser extent with the Rhodesian African Rifles. The rank and file of the RAR was black. There was some manipulation of this toward the end of the war, but broadly speaking the fact remained. The officer corps, on the other hand, was white. Efforts were made to introduce blacks into the officers mess toward the end of the war, but again, the fact remains.

The RAR operated as orthodox infantry in two battalions, tending on the whole to be locally deployed, but on one or two notable occasions the RAR was deployed on external operations. The unit was selectively parachute trained and was very frequently involved with internal Fire Force operations.

The general fighting capacity of the Rhodesian army was reinforced by two rear-echelon units, Guard Force and The Rhodesia Defence Regiment. The former was a modestly trained paramilitary unit established to garrison and defend the protected village programme, and later to guard and protect important installations. Guard Force was not a frontline unit, but it saw more than its fair share of action. Protected villages and associated keeps were frequent targets of guerrilla attacks, and numbers of Guard Force members have been listed in the Rhodesia roll of honour as killed in action.

The Rhodesia Defence Regiment was home to those non-blacks subject to conscription, but not deemed sufficiently reliable to be deployed to frontline combat units. Such would have been members of the local Asian and coloured communities, who tended to be the main fodder for the Rhodesia Defence Regiment. The RDR was usually to be found guarding bridges, railway stations, power installations, road works and any other item of infrastructure that required full-time security. Again, the RDR was not a frontline unit, but a number of notable actions were fought involving the RDR, and over the years of the war many casualties were recorded.

Internal Affairs, or Intaf, and also known as Lighthouse, was an effective evolution of the old Native Affairs administration of the colonial period. Although retaining much of that original identity, Internal Affairs represented community government within the native and agricultural areas. A province typically fell under the remit of a Provincial Commissioner (PC), who in turn oversaw the activities of a number of District Commissioners (DCs). Districts were served by District Officers (DOs), District Assistants (DAs) and District Messengers (DMs). All personnel above District Officer rank were white, and all below that rank tended to be black. By the mid-1970s Internal Affairs had adopted a paramilitary identity, and in effect had become a branch of the security forces. It worked in close cooperation with Guard Force in the administration and protection of the protected villages.

Armoured cars and artillery played a very limited role in the prosecution of the war. The Rhodesian Artillery Regiment, formed in 1964, utilized mainly the British Ordnance QF 25-pounder in an infantry support role, occasionally being involved in cross-border operations, but on the whole being limited by a conventional configuration in a counter-insurgency environment. Armoured cars also played a very limited role. The Rhodesian Armoured Corps suffered from low procurement priority, and as a

RAR soldiers advance through savannah country. *Source Masodja*

The RAR was selectively parachute trained. Here the paratroopers wait for an equipment check before emplaning. *Source Masodja*

consequence it was heir to a selection of ceremonial British Ferret armoured scout cars inherited from the Federal armed forces of the 1950s and early 1960s. South African Eland armoured cars, modelled closely on the French Panhard AML, eventually came into service toward the end of the war, and were used most notably in Selous Scouts' pseudo column operations into Mozambique. In October 1979 the Armoured Corps was gifted eight Polish-built T-55 tanks confiscated by the South Africans from a Libyan cargo ship en route to Angola. These arrived in Rhodesia too late to be of any material assistance to the prosecution of the war.

The glue that bound together all of the combined branches of the Rhodesian security forces was the Rhodesian Air Force (RhAF). This remarkable institution had been in existence in one form or another since the 1930s, evolving through induction into the Royal Air Force during the Second World War, and emerging as the Rhodesian Air Force only after the break up of the Central African Federation and the transfer of the bulk of federal air assets south to Rhodesia.

The backbone of the Rhodesian counter-insurgency response was its use of helicopters. The workhorse French Alouette III carried the heaviest load throughout the hard-fighting days of the war. The actual numbers of these in operation in Rhodesia varied according to South African willingness to make them available, but on average there were fifty operational machines in Rhodesia at any one time. The Zimbabwean government, when it assumed power, took over just eight functioning Alouette IIIs, the remainder had either been grounded or returned to South Africa.

Rhodesian strike capacity was provided by a squadron of Hawker Hunter FGA9 fighter-bombers that supported countless Fire Force operations during the course of the war, as well as being a major component in almost all the principal external raids. A heavier punch was delivered by a squadron of English Electric Canberra B2 and T4 light bombers, another consistent presence in the skies overhead as Rhodesian troops took the fight to the enemy in Mozambique and Zambia, flying on one notable mission as far as Vila Luso in Angola in order to deliver a payload over a known guerrilla training camp. This operation, codenamed Operation Vanity, was conducted alongside three SAAF Canberras on loan from South Africa, and South African pilots were both amazed and impressed at the ingenuity of Rhodesian pilots and crew in keeping these aging but irreplaceable aircraft in the air.

The RhAF also flew Vampire FB9s and two-seater T11s jets, Cessna 337 Skymaster* (Lynx) and Siai-Marchetti SF260 (Genet) propeller-driven strike aircraft. Provost T52s and the Vampires were used in a strike capacity during the early phase of the war, but were withdrawn to a training role toward the end of the 1970s.

The Rhodesian security forces were perpetually under-supplied and under-equipped thanks to international sanctions and an effective arms embargo, but despite this the war was sustained effectively throughout the period of greatest insecurity. A blend of ingenuity and marked superiority in leadership, tactics, organization and training all combined to give Rhodesian fighting forces a consistant edge over a numerically superior enemy. It has been said that no single tactical defeat was registered by the Rhodesian security forces, despite it ultimately losing the war, and although this is not strictly true, there certainly was no point at which the forces of the country were ever in danger of a military defeat, and no part of the country was ever inaccessible to Rhodesian forces. Rhodesia suffered a purely political defeat, attempting in a contemporary context to defend the indefensible.

---

* These were in fact Cessna 337FTBs as they were made under licence by Reims in France.

CHAPTER EIGHT:
AN ATTEMPT TO SETTLE MATTERS INTERNALLY

The result of John Vorster's and Henry Kissinger's diplomacy in Rhodesia was the Geneva conference that took place between October and December 1976. Neither side had an appetite for peace at that time. The Rhodesian delegation faced off with the Patriotic Front, a union of ZANU and ZAPU, imposed on the movement by the OAU, and which was almost completely dominated by Robert Mugabe. Joshua Nkomo was the senior nationalist, and the universally preferred candidate for power in a free Zimbabwe, but he was wholly eclipsed by the militant, aggressive and utterly uncompromising Mugabe.

ZANLA had opened 1976 with a tentative but nonetheless determined infiltration of the eastern third of Rhodesia. Mugabe's military philosophy was simple, to overrun Rhodesia with a human wave of sparsely trained and nominally equipped guerrilla units. These would be configured to attack soft targets, and in particular to render the rural and farming areas economically untenable. Targeting whites on the land would hit the Rhodesians where they were most vulnerable, which would so attenuate the reach of Rhodesian security forces that very quickly it would become unsustainable.

Mugabe's vulnerability lay in the extent to which Mozambican President Samora Machel would be prepared to absorb the economic cost of war with Rhodesia. Both Machel and his Frontline State colleague, Kenneth Kaunda of Zambia, had brought pressure to bear on their respective proxies in an effort to bring matters to an early conclusion. This was not very different from Ian Smith's own conundrum of having to dance to South African prime minister John Vorster's rather whimsical tune.

The timbre of negotiations in Geneva was prickly at best, and openly hostile for most of the time. Conference chairman Ivor Richards, a lowly ex-British ambassador to the United Nations, had quite clearly been plucked from the ranks and handed a poisoned chalice. The British at the highest level remained pessimistic and aloof. The Americans, now under the administration of Democrat Jimmy Carter, had deferred to British policy while Vorster had largely lost interest.

All parties to the conference went through the motions, but when on the evening of 20 December 1976, a ZANLA platoon entered the labour compound of the Aberfoyle Tea Estate in the Eastern Highlands of Rhodesia and gunned down twenty-seven men in front of their horrified families, the Rhodesians were served a perfect opportunity to plea the pointlessness of trying to deal with such a bunch of ruthless savages.

A satisfying international uproar was accompanied by tight-lipped silence from the Patriotic Front. Retribution meted out by the Rhodesian security forces, however, was as usual swift and effective. In internal counter-insurgency operations, 321 terrorists

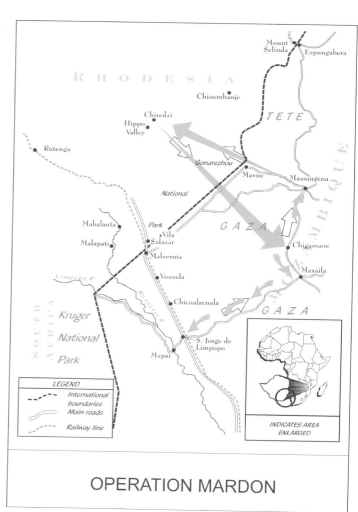

OPERATION MARDON

Source Genevieve Edwards

were killed. Externally, the SAS, the Selous Scouts and the RLI, launched Operation Mardon, a series of hard-hitting raids against targets in the Tete and Gaza provinces of Mozambique. A number of separate camps were taken out and large numbers of ZANLA personnel killed, for the loss of two Rhodesian soldiers. Huge quantities of weaponry were also recovered.

In a separate operation a combined SAS and RLI force neutralized Mavue base in Mozambique, killing 31 terrorists, and in early December a camp at Rambanayi in Mozambique was hit, severely mauling a platoon of Tanzanian troops stationed there. And in direct retaliation for the Aberfoyle killings, the SAS mounted a raid on the adjacent town of Mavonde in Mozambique which accounted for 44 members of ZANLA.

With this sort of thing going on in Rhodesia, the Geneva conference simply died of indifference. The parties broke for Christmas in December 1976 and simply never reconvened. The Nyadzonya raid of October 1976 had delivered ZANLA forces an extremely hard slap that had served clear notice of the fact that picking a fight with white Rhodesia would be a painful and costly affair, and the attacks that followed simply backed up this fact.

But nonetheless, as 1976 slipped into 1977, and as the year progressed, the military situation in Rhodesia deteriorated

The Rambanayi camp burns. Several Frelimo corpses can be seen lying in the dry riverbed.

Blowing the bridge at Rambanayi in an effort to prevent a Frelimo follow-up. The plan failed as hundreds of Frelimo troops mobilized from the neighbouring area and chased the Rhodesian forces back to the border.

13 Troop 3 Commando 1RLI mops up after the raid.

progressively. The steady emigration of whites out of the country, along with the vaulting escalation of hostile incursions, tended to underline the fact that Rhodesia was living on borrowed time. Almost half the annual Rhodesian defence bill was being picked up by South Africa, and without South African arms supplies and material support, collapse in Rhodesia would be almost immediate. So far no single foreign power had moved to recognize the rebel republic and the complacency and confidence of the 1960s slowly devolved into a desperation on the part of Ian Smith and his right-wing government to find a solution to the crisis.

Smith then began to look internally. White Rhodesia by then almost universally harboured a morbid fear of Robert Mugabe, thanks in large part to the unrestrained Marxist tone of his rhetoric and the angry violence of his anti-white attitude, all of which tended to promise the standards of lunatic government that was at that point epitomized by the sociopathic rule of the likes of Idi Amin in Uganda, Jean Bedel Bokassa in the Central African Republic and Francisco Macías Nguema of Equatorial Guinea. The political mantra in Rhodesia became one of avoiding dealing with Mugabe at all costs. Even Joshua Nkomo, with his comfort-loving venality and corruptibility, became a much more palatable option.

Smith, however, settled on two reasonable and extremely malleable nationalists around whom to create a moderate, internal nationalist bloc. These were Sithole, the original leader of ZANU, who now led a minority breakaway splinter of the party in the aftermath of his ousting by Mugabe, and Bishop Abel Muzorewa, who had come to political prominence as the head of the United African National Council that had been formed as a bulwark against the Pearce commission, and the 1971 political settlement. Muzorewa had originally been chosen to lead the UANC because he represented such an innocuous and unthreatening figure that white Rhodesia could hardly dissapprove. He had, however, in recent months developed something of an independent political ambition, and was now more than happy to entertain overtures from Ian Smith to serve as the acceptable face of Rhodesian black nationalism. The cost was entry into an internal agreement with the enemy, but the reward would be the premiership of an independent Zimbabwe, albeit by the back door.

On 24 November 1977, Smith made a formal announcement to the nation that he had invited three 'internal' black leaders—Muzorewa, Sithole and Chief Jeremiah Chirau—to the conference table. Almost as those words were being spoken, just about every portable Rhodesian security asset was being mobilized and directed toward one of the most spectacular external raids of the war so far.

CHAPTER NINE:
OPERATION DINGO

It is arguable that no single operation at any time during the Rhodesian war quite illustrated the capability and attitude of the Rhodesian security forces quite like Operation Dingo. Operation Mardon, undertaken between 30 October and 5 November 1976, and targeting ZANLA facilities in Mozambique's Tete, Manica, Sofala and Gaza provinces, had been undertaken largely to weaken the position of the Patriotic Front at the Geneva conference being held more or less at the same time. Mardon, and Operation Eland, the Selous Scouts strike against the Nydzonya camp in Mozambique, had set back ZANLA operations, but they did not halt them. The ZANLA high command simply made the decision to pull back closer to the city of Chimoio, the provincial capital of Manica province. This decision was made in the expectation that the distance from Rhodesia and the proximity to centres of population and large local Frelimo military bases would deter a repeat attack.

The Rhodesians, however, through regular aerial photography, maintained an ongoing surveillance on ZANLA activity in Mozambique. By the beginning of 1977, two significant ZANLA rear bases had been identified. These were New Farm, located on an abandoned farm about twelve miles northeast of Chimoio, and Tembué, sited significantly more remotely in the northern Tete province, tucked almost within the three corners of Mozambique, Malawi and Zambia, and really, for all intents and purposes, far beyond the reach of Rhodesian conventional capability.

New Farm served as the main ZANLA holding and training centre, handling the flow of recruits entering Mozambique from Rhodesia, and those trained cadres returning from instruction in China, Tanzania and Ethiopia. It was also home to ZANLA's operational, logistical and administrative headquarters, with offices for all the major figures in the movement, including Robert Mugabe. All ZANLA activities in the central Manica province were coordinated from here, along with the reinforcement, resupply and organization of guerrilla operations in eastern and southeastern Rhodesia. Estimates of camp occupation suggested a rotating population of upward of 4,000 trained and semi-trained personnel. New Farm was therefore a major target.

Tembué was somewhat less tempting. It held the ZANLA command headquarters for Tete province, and was home to some 2,000 cadres, serving a similar administrative and command-and-control function in the northeast operational areas of Rhodesia as New Farm did in the east.

Both camps were well defended and carefully structured to avoid the same concentrations of facilities and personnel that had made the Nydzonya attack so easy once the vehicles had managed to gain entry to the camp. New Farm comprised 17 camps, scattered over 25 square miles of territory. Likewise, Tembué had three dispersed camps along the east bank of the Luia river, a tributary of the Capoche river, itself a tributary of the Zambezi. Quite clearly, attempting to take out just one of these would be an operation that would be daring—bordering on reckless. Even taking into account the vast superiority of the Rhodesian security forces, the odds envisaged here were astronomical.

But nonetheless, the thought was pondered, by, among others, SAS commander Major Brian Robinson and air force Group Captain Norman Walsh, Director of Air Operations. Both men had, over several weeks, devised a blueprint for a daring joint air force and airborne SAS attack on New Farm, followed a day or so later by a similar assault against Tembué.

It is interesting to note here that the mythology of the Rhodesian war, never wholly reliable, has tended to suggest that the profes-

An SAS squadron at Lake Alexander, Operation Dingo Zulu 1's jump-off point.
Source Craig Fourie

Operation Dingo Zulu 1: Alouette's refuelling at the admin base inside Mozambique.

Three C-47 Dakotas en route to disgorge their paratroopers over the New Farm contact area during Operation Dingo.

RLI paratroop drop. *Source Max Tee*

sional rivalry that existed between the SAS and the Selous Scouts prompted Brian Robinson on behalf of his unit to devise something more spectacular and more dramatic than the Nyadzonya raid.

Brian Robinson had been summoned, alongside the Selous Scouts' commanding officer, Lieutenant-Colonel Ron Reid-Daly, to appear before the Operations Coordinating Committee to comment on the feasibility of an attack against Nyadzonya, and he had written it off as impossible.

As history would prove, the Selous Scouts gave clear notice of the fact that an operation against Nyadzonya camp was eminently possible. Even after the spectacular success of the attacks against New Farm and Tembué, Nydzonya remains, arguably, the signature Rhodesian cross-border operation of the war, defined by the daring and audacity that Rhodesians so cherished about their own legend.

Despite this, there was a great deal of caution at the higher command level when the plan was first presented. This was premised primarily on the enormous military risks involved—it must be remembered that any Rhodesian personnel or equipment loss was highly impactful. But also the likely international political fallout that would accrue from the operation the moment

the ZANU propaganda machine sought to betray the target as an innocent civilian refugee camp, which it would do no matter what the material circumstances.

During the latter half of 1977, several versions of the plan were submitted. By then the RLI had been parachute trained, which expanded the pool of manpower available for the assault, coupled with the fact that the concentration and expansion of both ZANLA camps left no doubt about that fact that one way or another this dangerous build-up of force needed to be dealt with. The catalysts for a breakthrough was the collapse of an Anglo-American peace initiative. Smith had been hampered and frustrated by ongoing fruitless and unnecessary political interference, but after the Geneva conference, and the Kissinger phase of international diplomacy, he found that he had a freer hand.

This presented Smith with the opportunity to plunge into his strategy of grooming a handful of moderate internal national-ists—Bishop Abel Muzorewa (UANC) and Ndabaningi Sithole (ZANU) primary among them—to contest an election based on a revised constitution, opening the electorate to universal adult suf-frage.* The constitution would be put to the current, largely white electorate for approval, after which the expectation would be that Rhodesia would have a black prime minister, heavily circumscribed by residual power maintained very much in white hands, but none-theless presenting the image of majority rule. Smith hoped that this would undermine the position of Robert Mugabe, who had emerged as the man most to be feared by white Rhodesia.

It was Smith's intention to announce this arrangement to the Rhodesian public late in November 1977, but before he did he authorized Operation Dingo, the combined assault against New Farm and Tembué, hoping, perhaps, that a two-pronged political and military assault against Robert Mugabe would precipitate a collapse of ZANU and a general recognition internationally of the Rhodesian internal settlement. D-Day was set for Wednesday 23 November 1977.

---

* Sithole had been ousted by Mugabe as the leader of ZANU, but he retained the name, later reinventing the party as ZANU Ndonga.

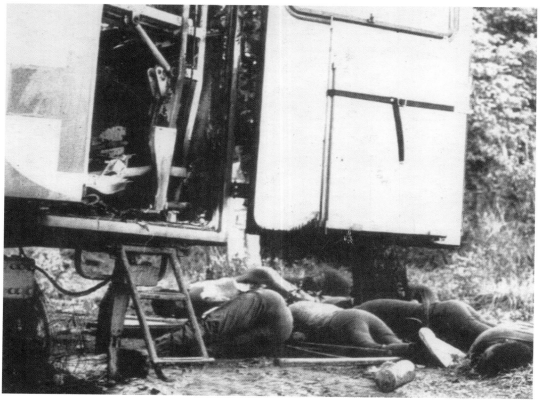

The aftermath of Operation Dingo. *Source Zimbabwean Ministry of Information*

Operation Dingo was divided into two parts, Zulu 1 (New Farm) and Zulu 2 (Tembué), both essentially comprising amplified Fire Force-style operations, and both involving a blistering air assault, utilizing almost every appropriate asset of the RhAF, followed up by the deployment of SAS and RLI troops in stop groups to intercept ZANLA cadres who, after the air assault, could be relied upon to be fleeing in all directions. These would be dealt with efficiently and ruthlessly by troops well versed in the tactic by then. Thereafter, mopping-up would involve flushing out die-hard elements and suppressing any entrenched resistance within the camp complex. Large quantities of intelligence material and captured ordnance could be expected at the end of the operation.

Troops were deployed both by helicopter and parachute drop, again utilizing every troop-carrying asset available to Rhodesia at the time, leaving very little scope for rescue in the event of a catastrophic failure. Planning that had been undertaken over several months was fine-tuned in the few days between clearance and execution, in the fervent hope that nothing catastrophic would occur—and indeed it did not.

The assault was spearheaded by sanctions-busting air legend Captain Jack Malloch. His role would be to fly his commercial Douglas DC-8 cargo liner at height over the morning muster parades to mask the noise of the Rhodesian air armada to within earshot. And this was precisely what happened.

Thereafter, an almost textbook operation rolled out. Reports vary at the number of casualties achieved in this operation, but Group Captain Peter Petter-Boyer, a recognized authority on Rhodesian air operations, estimates that up to 3,000 ZANU combatants were killed, and as many as 5,000 wounded in both phases

of Operation Dingo. As the Rhodesians wrapped up the first phase and headed home, they returned with two dead and six injured.

An inevitable hue and cry followed as preparations quietly went ahead for Zulu 2, prompting British Secretary of State for Foreign and Commonwealth Affairs, David Owen, to remark that, whatever else the attack might have represented, it served clear notice of the fact that the Rhodesian security forces were not on their back, as many claimed. And indeed this was true. The operation in its first phase had stretched Rhodesian capability to its limit, but it proved unequivocally that there where some sharp kicks left in the dying Rhodesian donkey, and that those predicting a military defeat in Rhodesia need do so with extreme caution.

The second phase of the operation, Zulu 2, went ahead as planned, and although somewhat less spectacularly successful, was nonetheless another textbook exercise in the planning and execution of a Fire Force raid.

In the meanwhile, the internal political process progressed smoothly against this backdrop of a hot war. On the morning of Friday 3 March 1978, the parties to the internal settlement gathered at Governor's House in Salisbury and signed into being an accord between the white-dominated government of Rhodesia and the internal nationalists.

The agreement was defined by a new constitution that would allow for universal suffrage and the election of a majority-rule government. This would, in practical terms, hand the superficial accoutrements of power to whosoever would win the election, confidently predicted to be Bishop Abel Muzorewa and his UANC party, while at the same time retaining the real instruments of power—defence and control of the civil service—in white hands.

In his cabinet announcement of 30 May 1979, Prime Minister Abel Muzorewa retained the portfolios of combined operations and defence for himself. In practice, however, he had little real authority over the armed forces, for all senior appointments were still held by whites who owed allegiance to the Rhodesian Front party rather than to a black government. On the very day that Muzorewa was sworn into office Smith established an unofficial war council comprising Lieutenant-General Peter Walls, the chiefs of the army and air force, the commissioner of police and the Director General of the CIO.

CHAPTER TEN:
THE CLOSING STAGES

If any indication was needed of the sheer futility of this exercise, it was perhaps best manifest by the events of 23 June 1978. On the evening of that day, a group of ZANLA guerrillas entered the Elim Pentecostal Mission, located some twenty kilometres outside the border town of Umtali in the lovely scenic backdrop of the Vumba mountains. The events of that night would both scar and disgust the nation, and to many determined sceptics on the outside, it would at last bring home some of the raw facts of this dirty little war.

Since the first instances of insecurity in Rhodesia in the 1960s, there had been a sub-strata of brutality in this war that many within Rhodesia took as clear evidence of the fact that the blacks had no business aspiring to govern a civilized state.

While this might have been a view somewhat selectively expressed, it can never be said that it was entirely based on a fallacy. The revised strategy that had been rolled out in the early 1970s by both nationalist parties comprised a heady propaganda synthesis of Marxism, local lore and tribal mythology, all leavened with a significant recall of the First Chimurenga of 1896, and stiffly reinforced by the application of shocking levels of violence and atrocity.

The latter was in order that it be generally understood that betrayal of the revolution would carry with it extremely severe penalties. Any suggestion of an individual or a community being sympathetic to the government was simply an invitation to horrific reprisals that were limited only by the imagination of individual guerrilla groups.

The more mundane versions of this involved simple shooting or bayoneting to death, but more creative political enforcement sometimes included the burning to death of families in grass huts, the cutting off of ears and lips and other acts of brutality that often escaped international censure only thanks to the general unpopularity of reporting negatively about any guerrilla activity.

Most of the extreme violence perpetrated during the war was black on black. Although a great many whites were murdered at the hands of ZANLA or ZIPRA guerrilla, very few suffered the barbarity that was most often reserved for blacks. It is also true that most black civilians were unarmed, while there were very few white civilians who were not extremely well protected by multiple layers of personal and homestead security. However, large numbers of whites still died as a consequence of roadside ambushes and landmines, and many just by being in the wrong place at the wrong time.

But pinning down and killing an armed white Rhodesian was often a tricky thing to do, but not so the missionaries. Rural missions, many of whom retained white missionaries throughout the war, were always a soft target. Few, if any were armed, or

A Selous Scouts tracking team.

would accept government protection for fear of being seen to be taking sides. On Sunday 6 February 1977, a group of armed men arrived in the compound of St Paul's Roman Catholic Mission in Musami, about fifty kilometres east of Salisbury, and marched nine members of the white clerical staff—three of whom were women—out into the open where they were shot. A month after the St Paul's incident, two white Roman Catholic missionaries, both women, were shot dead by guerrillas.

At the end of September however, a white population growing increasingly desensitized to reports of violent death, were shocked anew to open their newspapers and read a report on the senseless murder in Chipinga of six-month-old Natasha Glenny. The baby had been bayoneted to death while tethered to the back of her black nanny, who at first tried to hide her, and then said that she was her own albino child.

However, nothing quite touched the sense of hopelessness beginning to take root in the collective heart of white Rhodesia than the atrocity perpetrated at the Elim Mission in June 1978. On the evening of the 8th, a group of guerrillas entered the mission precincts and instructed the black students of the school to pack up their belongings and repair to their quarters, because the school would be closing down.* From there the white British expatriate staff, comprising three male and four female missionaries along with four children, were rounded up and escorted to the playing fields where they were summarily beaten and bayoneted to death. One woman, 28-year-old Mary Fisher, survived her beating and a variety of stab wounds, after which she crawled into the bush where she was found the following morning by security force details. She died later at the Andrew Fleming Hospital in Salisbury.

For some time the bodies were left where they had fallen in order that the full impact of the night's horror could be recorded by the international press. The Rhodesian foreign minister personally accompanied a batch of journalists who had been hurriedly mustered by the ministry of information to the scene of the atrocity, and the gruesome scenes shortly thereafter appeared on the front pages of newspapers and journals around the world.

An interesting epilogue here, as it was with the St Paul's massacre, and many other particularly heinous atrocities committed by guerrilla units, was an attempt by the ZANLA high command and political leadership to blame the action on the Selous Scouts.

Why this is interesting is because the Selous Scouts were

---

* Elim Mission was located in what had been a private boys' school called Eagle School that had closed down as a consequence of insecurity.

without doubt responsible for some level of killings and atrocities in their prosecution of the war. The Selous Scouts, it must be remembered, was divided into two distinct facets. The first, and original, was the pseudo–tracking arm of the unit, which made significant use of turned guerrillas, and a more conventionally configured infantry special-force arm used primarily in the pseudo column external operations.

Of the former, many members were simply plucked from the ranks of ZANLA or ZIPRA, and with a minimum of formality, turned for operation in the Selous Scouts. Therefore many guerrilla tactics were transplanted into the day-to-day practice of the Selous Scouts, even if this was not part of the operational procedure of the regiment. In order to appear to be authentic, pseudo guerrillas were often required to do what authentic guerrillas would do, and if this required a certain amount of gratuitous killing and violence, then quite often this did take place.

The matter was never entirely resolved, although written notes found on the body of a ZANLA guerrilla killed some time later tended to implicate ZANLA in the killings as a revenge action against the attacks of Chimoio and Tembué, and in fact in practical terms there has never been any real doubt that elements of ZANLA were responsible.

CHAPTER ELEVEN:
STRATEGIES AND COMMAND STRUCTURES

On the evening of 3 September 1978, a Russian Strela SAM-7 missile brought down Air Rhodesia Vickers Viscount *Hunyani* soon after its take off from Kariba airport. Flight 825 took a direct hit on the heat exchanger–jet pipe assembly that knocked out both starboard engines. As the passengers for the most part maintained their composure, the pilot struggled to control the stricken aircraft long enough to bring it down in an open field in the Urungwe Tribal Trust Land, killing 35 of the 53 passengers aboard. Ten survivors were later murdered on the ground by a ZIPRA unit deployed in the vicinity to mop up survivors. Because this aircraft was overbooked, a second Viscount was lined up for take-0off with General Peter Walls on board. It has often been suggested that it was he who was the principal target of the attack.

The Viscount *Hunyani* incident—the shooting down as an act of war of a civilian airliner—attracted surprisingly little international condemnation once the news had broken. The effect of this on Rhodesian morale was ruinous, but it also had the effect of serving notice that ZIPRA had acquired, and was using, sophisticated Soviet weapons' systems.

In fact, since the catastrophic split in the ZAPU leadership that had almost brought the whole nationalist movement down with it, ZAPU had undergone extensive reorganization under the leadership of Jason Moyo. A consultative conference was held in 1976 that established the existence of ZIPRA, or the Zimbabwe People's Revolutionary Army, along with formulating its basic

command structures and strategies.

ZAPU had missed the opportunity to take advantage of the opening up of the Mozambique front, thanks to the implosion of the party in the early 1970s, which had given ZANU a significant military advantage to complement the massive leadership advantage that had accrued once Robert Mugabe had assumed control of the party.

It is not necessary here to review in detail the restructuring of ZAPU in response to the amplified conditions of war, other than taking note of the fact that responsibility for military policy and administration was placed in the hands of a secretary for defence. Command functions were carried out by ZIPRA commander, Lookout Masuku, a 31-year-old foreign-trained veteran, and a charismatic and intuitive military commander.

Masuku headed the ZIPRA high command, which comprised him and his deputies, other chiefs and deputies of departments, including artillery, communications, logistics, medical services, operations, personnel and training and reconnaissance and transport. Immediately below these were frontline commanders and their deputies, rear-camp commanders and their deputies, and of course the National Security Organization, or NSO structure.

The NSO was the internal security and intelligence arm of ZAPU, which was headed by Dumiso Dabengwa, an impressive 32-year-old ex-guerrilla who was one of the first to receive foreign military training. The role of the NSO, besides its security and

One fewer anti-aircraft gun to worry about. Captured weapons were put to good use in airfield defence.

The *Hunyani* and *Umniati* Viscount incidents were a grim reminder that in modern warfare there are no civilians.

intelligence functions, was to keep the war council up to date with intelligence and research briefings, and to present strategic option proposals for the consideration of the war council.

It can be clearly seen from this that ZAPU was assuming a noticeably more orthodox and conventional configuration, as opposed to the highly politicized Maoist concept of a protracted people's war that had been adopted by both ZANLA and Frelimo in Mozambique. The Revolutionary Council of ZAPU examined more closely the model of Vietnamese People's Army commander-in-chief Võ Nguyên Giáp, who postulated a three-stage strategy of guerrilla war. The first was a period of gestation, during which the outnumbered and outgunned guerrilla forces developed their rural bases from where the process of mass political mobilization was begun. The second stage was reached when the logistical and intelligence networks established by the guerrillas began to challenge those of the enemy, after which a brief period of power symmetry would be reached. From this the guerrilla forces would be poised to move on to stage three, which would see the deployment of large-scale mobile warfare campaigns leading eventually, it could be assumed, to a final offensive. It was this later phase that began increasingly to preoccupy the leadership of ZAPU as it built up its conventional military capacity under the tutelage of its Soviet advisers.

As a consequence, alongside its orthodox guerrilla units operational in the field, ZIPRA set about selectively enlisting personnel with the capacity to be trained in conventional and semi-conventional tactics. At the same time, an arsenal of sophisticated armaments was being assembled, including recoilless artillery, tanks and aircraft, as well as the Strela shoulder-fired heat-seeking missiles that had brought down the Air Rhodesia Viscount, all of which where supplied by the Russians. Units were upgraded into

brigade and detachment formations with a view to preparing them for conventional military assaults. Commanders were coached to lead from the front and ZIPRA units were to be despatched into the field with the advantage of mobile communications equipment.

The apparent strategy for dealing with ZANLA was to allow ZANLA within the areas it dominated to break the back of the Rhodesian security forces, and then to attack ZANLA in a conventional capacity at the point of white surrender, using its superior mobile capability to then seize territory, occupy it and defend it.

ZANLA did not appear to enjoy a particularly high standard of military leadership, and nor any inspired military tactics. Mugabe placed a great deal of emphasis on the war, and was known to prefer the option of an outright military solution, but was in general disinterested in military affairs and certainly cared very little for the well-being or fate of the warriors. Since ZANU enjoyed the support of the majority Chishona-speaking peoples of Zimbabwe, it could count on the mass mobilization of force and, backed up by Chinese arms supplies, it was able to apply a human-wave philosophy that relied on large numbers of nominally trained cadres deployed over a wide area to overwhelm the capacity of the Rhodesian security forces to respond.

ZANLA appeared to envisage a zero-hour scenario that would involve a collapse of the Rhodesian military capacity coupled with the holding of large areas of liberated territory that would position it to assume power as a consequence of its status as a popular movement.

The definition of a liberated zone in the ZANLA lexicon was an area or region that had fallen under the substantive control of the revolution, which in the context of the Rhodesian war never happened. There were many areas that might have been regarded as contested zones, but liberated zones did not exist. Nonetheless, the strategy of small-unit incursion, preceded by politicization and arms caching was extremely effective in attenuating and overwhelming Rhodesian military capacity. But no definitive zero-hour strategy existed to seize power militarily, leading to the supposition that the ZANU political ideology envisaged a negotiated surrender prior to a total military defeat. In real terms, taking into account the geopolitical realities of southern Africa at that time, this was both a sensible and pragmatic position.

The Rhodesian command and control structure was configured on standard British lines, with high command variations specifically configured to suit the precise operational conditions of the theatre. It is impossible to complete any of the many memoirs and histories of Rhodesian military operations without unearthing some deep-seated discontent over the inefficiencies and shortfalls of Rhodesian operational command.

The most common complaint levelled by those falling under the command structure of the Rhodesian security forces, and attempting to plan and execute operations, was, on the one hand, that it had not evolved effectively beyond the requirements of the pre-1972 security demands, and that on the whole it was uncoordinated and ill conceived.

At the start of the insurgency in 1965, it was understood that the army was in support of the police, and not vice versa. This continued to be more or less understood, notwithstanding the fact that operations tended to emphasize a military rather than police doctrine in counter-insurgency. This was certainly the case up until 1972, when the first permanent JOC, Operation Hurricane, was established in the northeast. The official Rhodesian Army definition of a Joint Operations Centre is as follows: "A joint agency set up by the security forces on the authority of government for the conduct of operations when no single service is solely responsible."

A JOC consisted of the senior BSAP, army, Special Branch and air force officers present, along with the appropriate commissioner of the department of Internal Affairs. Since the army representative tended to be the highest-ranking officer, it was usually he who assumed chairmanship of the JOC at the start of operations. Operation Hurricane was established at brigade level, with the headquarters of 2 Brigade moving from Salisbury, first to Centenary and then to Bindura.

By 1979 the entire country had fallen under five major operational areas, and these, alongside Hurricane, were codenamed Thrasher, Repulse, Tangent and Grapple. There were a number of sub-JOCs associated with each of these. There were initially three brigade headquarters—1 Brigade Bulawayo, 2 Brigade Salisbury and 3 Brigade Umtali. A fourth brigade headquarters, 4 Brigade, was later headquartered in Fort Victoria. In addition there was a maritime operational area, Operation Splinter, centred on Lake Kariba, and SALOPS, a police-controlled area concerned with Salisbury and surrounds.

In 1964, an Operations Coordinating Committee was established to coordinate and approve combined operations.

In 1977, with the quickening pace of the war, and calls for a more centralized command structure, a ministry of combined operations was formed, and a war council revived. The former was overseen by a minister of combined operations, and a military commander of combined operations was appointed in the person of army commander Lieutenant-General Peter Walls, who at the time was shortly due to retire under the terms of army regulations, and who then, in effect, became the central command personality in all military operations.

Walls was answerable to the minister of combined operations, creating a more centralized command structure, but also a more politically sensitive vehicle for the interpretation of the decisions of government into effective military strategy.

The main advantage achieved by this centralization of command was in stiffening the informality of liaison that had previously been both the main strength and the principal weakness of the Joint Operations Centre structure. Previous arrangements had seen issues affecting JOCs and sub-JOCs routed by the representatives of the various components of the JOCs—army and air force, police, intelligence and Internal Affairs—through their own ministerial channels prior to any centralized command element.

According to the official announcement, the commander of combined operations, Lieutenant-General Peter Walls would have command authority over all elements of the security forces, as well as any civil agencies—police and Internal Affairs primarily—directly engaged in the prosecution of operations against insurgent forces. This included direct command of special forces and special-force operations, including Selous Scouts, SAS, PATU and Grey's Scouts, which, in effect, left very little operational command in the hands of the army commander, General John Hickman, other than administrative and logistical responsibilities for the army as a whole, and direct command only of territorial operations and the Rhodesian African Rifles.

This had the inevitable effect of creating a certain amount of hostility between these two fundamentally separate command entities, and of course between Hickman and Walls themselves. ComOps—General Walls in effect—had gained direct control over the operational planning functions of the various services without incorporating their various planning staffs, so the complications were potentially manifold, with each service required to do its own logistical planning, which, with persistent manpower shortages, hardly made optimum use of resources.

The general complaint levelled at the Rhodesian military command structure, and the conduct of the war as a whole, has tended to be that the war was fought with an excessive emphasis on the role of the military in dealing with a fundamentally political situation, and not enough recognition of the associated socio-economic and racial realities that underwrote the war. This tended to negate the emergence of a rational and holistic strategy to fight the war, coupled with an excess of political interference in military conduct, which created a great deal of confusion and unnecessary squandering of resources, as well as the general misdirection of energy.

CHAPTER TWELVE:
REVENGE ATTACKS AND COMPROMISES

Prior to the downing of the Air Rhodesia Viscount, ZIPRA had tended to be given a lower operational priority than ZANLA. Most of the high-profile external operations so far had been focused on ZANLA bases and facilities in Mozambique. The Viscount disaster, however, brought ZIPRA very much into the Rhodesian crosshairs. Not only had ZIPRA drawn attention to itself by shooting down a civilian airliner, but it was also becoming increasingly conspicuous thanks to the development of its conventional capacity, and the large-scale massing of equipment and personnel at various key points in Zambia.

There had been ongoing disruptive operations underway against ZIPRA and Zambian positions north of the Zambezi for most of 1978, but ZIPRA had so far been spared the sort of heavy punishment that was being fairly regularly delivered to ZANLA, and to Mozambique. This, however, was about to come to an end.

At that point both the CIO and the Selous Scouts had intelligence agents operational in Lusaka, and from these sources an accurate picture of ZIPRA strengths and placements was beginning to emerge.

The ZIPRA high command had observed and absorbed the lessons that were to be learned by ZANLA's experience in Mozambique. As a consequence the organization was very careful to site its main training and logistics bases out of the reach of Rhodesian attack.

The most important ZIPRA facility in Zambia was Freedom Camp, located on an abandoned farm some ten miles north of Lusaka, which was in practical terms beyond the scope of any Fire Force-type attack. This was thanks primarily to the camp's proximity to the Zambian capital, and Zambian army and air force placements. It was understood that upward of 4,000 ZIPRA personnel were present at Freedom Camp at any given time. It was also the home of ZIPRA's military high command, in effect its main planning and logistics facility and general HQ. As such it was a choice target, but in recognition of the risk of attempting a ground assault, Freedom Camp was earmarked for a dedicated RhAF assault.

In addition to Freedom Camp, ZIPRA had located several of its satellite installations far enough away from the Rhodesian border to place them beyond the capacity of the Rhodesians to deal with in a combined assault. Bearing in mind ZIPRA's conventional strategy, the distances between the bulk of ZIPRA forces and the Rhodesian border meant that any large-scale overland movement of men and equipment to the border could easily be frustrated. The Rhodesians, of course, took advantage of this opportunity the following year with a series of attacks that decimated the Zambian transport infrastructure through the demolition of key road and railway bridges. This, in a few well-timed and well-conceived manoeuvres, very effectively frustrated ZIPRA's short-term ability to mobilize.

However, for the moment the Rhodesians were interested in achieving two objectives. The first was to punish ZIPRA for its actions seven weeks earlier in bringing down Flight 825, and second to bring it home to President Kenneth Kaunda that the Rhodesian war had arrived on his soil in a major way.

The plan of operations followed very much the pattern already established. An air assault would be launched against Freedom Camp, utilizing helicopter gunships, fighter–bombers and bombers, followed by a return to Rhodesia for refuelling and rearming before a similar assault would be launched against a smaller ZIPRA facility located at Mkushi, some 100 miles northeast of Lusaka, thought to contain upward of 1,000 enemy combatants. After the initial aerial assault, an attack force of 120 SAS paratroopers, supported by a further 45 heliborne SAS troops, including an 81mm mortar team, would conduct a vertical envelopment that would mop up as many survivors of the initial attack as possible, after which the camp would be comprehensively destroyed.

To round off the day a third attack would be launched against what had been named ZIPRA's CGT-2 (Communist Guerrilla Training) camp, located about 60 miles east of Lusaka, and involving an air element of Vampire jets, Lynx and K-Car helicopter gunships, followed by a vertical envelopment by RLI parachute and heliborne troops to complete the operation.

The attacks went in on 19 October 1978, with the greatest concern being the possibility of the Zambian Air Force responding to the presence of Rhodesian air assets operating in Zambian air space, as well as the presence within Zambia at unknown locations of British Rapier surface-to-air missile systems.* It was decided that the lead Canberra would circle Lusaka International Airport, having delivered a pre-prepared message to air traffic control, warning that Rhodesian Hunters were poised to shoot down any Zambian aircraft with hostile intentions.

This was the iconic *Green Leader* incident that to an ostensibly critical world both indicated the hopeless inadequacy of black African military capacity, but also the indomitable spirit of white Rhodesia. The sheer audacity of an antiquated Rhodesian aircraft dictating to Zambia the terms of its own air-space usage for the period of the Freedom Camp attack warmed the hearts of a beleaguered white population.

Green Leader Message to Air Traffic Control Lusaka

GL.: Lusaka tower, this is Green Leader.

---

* The Zambian Air Force possessed an unknown number of serviceable Mig-17 and Mig-19 strike aircraft.

Lusaka tower: Station calling tower?

G.L.: Tower this is Green Leader. This is a message for the Station Commander at Mumbwa from the Rhodesian Air Force. We are attacking the terrorist base at Westlands Farm at this time. The attack is against Rhodesian dissidents and not against Zambia. Rhodesia has no quarrel, repeat no quarrel with Zambia or her security forces. We therefore ask you not to intervene or oppose our attack. However, we are orbiting your airfield at this time, and are under orders to shoot down any Zambian Air Force aircraft which does not comply with this request and attempts to take off. Did you copy all that?

Lusaka tower: Copied!

G.L.: Roger, thanks. Cheers!

The most reliable list of ZIPRA casualties recoded for that day was that presented to the Pan African Congress held in Tanzania that year, stating, probably conservatively, a tally of 396 killed, 719 injured and 192 missing, all at the cost of one Rhodesian SAS trooper fatally injured at Mkushi, and a helicopter destroyed where it crash landed in Zambia.

Despite the continuing success of the these daring external operations, the internal political settlement continued to yield disappointing results. As the deadline for the first majority-rule election drew near, the hard-line guerrilla elements allied to ZIPRA and ZANLA continued their defiance. This continued to undermine any potential for general recognition, and as such it continued to underline Robert Mugabe's military agenda.

By 1979, guerrilla incursions into Rhodesia had reached every sector of the country. Each JOC meeting reviewed the depressing reality of intelligence reports indicating increasing gains by large guerrilla groups now able to infiltrate across the long frontier more or less unmolested. Significant portions of the country had become no-go areas where security forces entered only on specific operations, or remained secure within fortified positions. The operational areas acquired nicknames like Operation *Thrashed* and *Repulsed*, reflecting the current mood of defeatism rife in the country.

By then active infiltration had taken place into the towns and cities. On the evening of 7 September 1978, the city of Umtali experienced a second mortar and rocket attack from positions inside Mozambique that injured four people.* A few weeks later a third 40-minute bombardment saw 150 projectiles of various sorts landing in scattered locations throughout the municipal area. It was the loudest and most sustained attack against the city so far.

Then, on 11 December 1978, a unit of six ZANLA combatants successfully penetrated the Salisbury industrial quarter and fired several RPG-7 rockets into the bulk fuel-storage containers. This caused a gargantuan explosion, and an ensuing blaze that, over the course of a week, consumed several months' supply of precious fuel.

All of this was indicative of the fact that the partners to

An RLI trooper inspects a ZIPRA bunker during the cross-border raid on ZIPRA's CGT-2 camp in Zambia. *Source Chris Cocks*

the internal settlement, Sithole and Muzorewa in particular, fundamentally did not command the loyalty of the main armed factions. Amnesty appeals had been issued, offering excellent terms of surrender to those active guerrillas who would surrender and swear loyalty to one or other of the internal nationalists. A few did, but a very few. Despite the fact that both main liberation movements made it known through a few salutary killings what the consequences of disloyalty would be, there was no authentic interest on either side because, in all probability, both sides, and very likely the Rhodesian side too, recognized that the entire enterprise had been a desperate gambit on the eve of defeat with absolutely no real chance of it succeeding.

Nonetheless, a plan was hatched under instructions from Lieutenant-General Peter Walls for the Selous Scouts to undertake a pseudo operation with a difference. Operation Favour involved the posing of Selous Scouts pseudo operatives as authentic guerrillas coming in from the bush under the terms of amnesty. This was in order to lend the impression that large numbers of ZANLA and ZIPRA fighters were indeed heeding the call. Both Muzorewa and Sithole were mandated to add to these their own core of armed supporters, and since neither man had anything resembling a solid corps of armed support, both hastily recruited from the streets and other sources. This led to the evolution of a politically ticklish, and tactically low-level force of men who were armed and nominally trained by the Rhodesian security forces.

---

* The first attack took place on 11 August 1976.

The Salisbury fuel depot ablaze, courtesy of ZANLA commandos.

In due course these became a significant but largely unreliable branch of the security forces known as Security Force Auxiliaries (SFAs). The SFAs were deployed into the countryside to represent the armed wings of Sithole's ZANU and Muzorewa's UANC.

The SFA's were given the name Spear of the People, or *Pfumo re Vhanu* in Chishona and *Umkonto wa Bantu* in Sindebele. A spear and shield emblem was assigned that was worn on brown, South African-supplied battle fatigues. By the end of the transition, the Spear of the People had become more or less an orthodox military formation comprising upward of 10,500 men.

ZANLA in particular went to great length to expose this ruse and punish its participants. A group of authentic ZANLA guerrillas waylaid two Security Force Auxiliaries in the Wedza TTL after they strayed from their group in search of alcohol and women. The two were then 'turned' and sent back to call the rest of the unit on the pretext that the ZANLA detachment wanted to surrender. A short while later a large group of auxiliaries walked into a well-laid trap. They were disarmed and their hands wired behind their backs. Since it was quite clear what was planned, a good many were able to run and lose themselves in the bush. Forty-one of their number, however, were executed on the spot and their bodies left on the side of the road as a lesson to their comrades.

Operationally the SFA programme was a disaster. Although garnished with military apparel and armed with Portuguese-manufactured G3 rifles, the new operatives had not been effectively re-educated, and—almost to a man—they retained their original loyalties. Because the unit was essentially made up of urban riff-raff, these loyalties were mainly to themselves. However, those who were originally aligned to ZANLA or ZIPRA tended to retain that alliance and desertions were commonplace. Security force details were increasingly reporting fleeting contacts with guerrilla groups, among which were men using both G3 and FN rifles.

Among those SFAs ostensibly loyal to Sithole was a group that had been for some time under training in Uganda. Uganda at this time was under the sway of Idi Amin, so the standard and bias of that training can easily be imagined. Upon their return to Rhodesia to be absorbed into Sithole's force, the group was armed and deployed into the Gokwe area in the north–central region of Rhodesia. There they very quickly began to show high levels of indiscipline and a marked reluctance to integrate, and it eventually became necessary to deal with them.

The task of taking care of this problem was given to C Company 10RR, in one of the less palatable operations of the Rhodesian war.

An instruction was issued that all SFAs were to muster at a local airfield in order to begin training in driving and MAG use in order that the army might issue light machine guns and vehicles to the unit. The plan then was to quietly surround the airfield, and at a given point a circling aircraft would proclaim via a sky shout that the entire group was under arrest.

This was Plan A. Much thought and preplanning went into its execution, but in respect of the fact that there were a great many variables to consider, Plan B was somewhat simpler. Should matters not proceed as planned, all the SFAs involved would be considered to be terrorists to be dealt with accordingly.

Such being the fog of war, Plan A did indeed begin to unravel very quickly. The news of the pending muster was greeted in the SFA camp with a great deal of scepticism, with the result that only some 130 of the 350 SFAs reported as instructed, and all who did arrived bristling with suspicion and unwilling to relinquish their weapons. Thirty or so detached themselves from the main group, and along with their weapons took cover in a building situated some 100 metres distant from the camp. The remaining 100 or so men moved cautiously onto the airstrip, all carrying their personal weapons.

As this was taking place a number of heavy vehicles arrived on the scene and encircled the airfield. These were ostensibly to be used for driving lessons, and each was equipped with a mounted light machine gun to lend the impression that fire drill was also intended. In due course a sky-shout aircraft arrived overhead and delivered an inaudible message that ended with the abrupt proclamation: "SFA, lay down your arms, you are under arrest."

The result was instant panic and a withering enfilade unleashed by the mounted MAGs. Those SFAs that survived and fled the initial carnage were dealt with at the edge of the airstrip as they ran into carefully placed stop groups. Killed also was the (Sithole) ZANU political commissar who had been party to the deception.

Those SFAs who had occupied the building on the edge of camp were immediately alerted and opened fire. The attention of the security forces was then focused on this location, which, after a fierce fire ight, was cleared, and all those sheltered within it killed. The bodies of those killed were hurriedly removed from the scene and buried in a mass grave. The details of this incident only came to light recently with a statement made by the commanding officer of C Company 10RR in the compiling of material for a history of the Rhodesia Regiment.

CHAPTER THIRTEEN:
CLOSING OPERATIONS AND THE POLITICS OF DEFEAT

The death of white Rhodesia came about as a consequence of two fundamental realities. The first was the fact that white rule in Africa had for over a decade been an obvious anachronism—obvious by the end of the 1970s even to a majority of southern African whites themselves—and the second was the steady haemorrhaging of reliable manpower as whites voted with their feet and left. By the late 1970s it had become manifestly clear that Rhodesia had its back against the wall. No nation on earth, not even South Africa, had officially recognized either Rhodesian independence or the internal settlement. The war had spread to every corner of the country, and many men were on almost permanent call-up. The RLI, consistently operating under strength, had begun to induct national service personnel. Moves were afoot to form a third battalion of the RAR and large number of AS (African Soldiers) were being used to flesh out the Rhodesia Regiment territorial battalions. The independent companies had been rebadged RAR, and were now utilizing black conscripts and other AS.

All of this, for primarily ideological reasons, represented a fatal weakening of the structure, serving clear notice that if a viable political solution were not found to the crisis, sooner rather than later, then the entire edifice was in danger of collapse.

Despite these facts, the cutting edge of the Rhodesian security forces was still effective and still deadly, and the closing operations of the war proved this fact eloquently.

The attention being given to Zambia continued with a series of operations undertaken by the SAS to compromise the ability of ZIPRA to mobilize against Rhodesia in a meaningful way. A dual purpose was, of course, to let it be known to Kenneth Kaunda that the price of ongoing war with Rhodesia would be punitive, and to encourage him to apply pressure to Joshua Nkomo to support an early compromise.

Such was the case also with Mozambique. The last major attacks launched into Mozambique have become iconic chapters in the ongoing histories of all the units involved, primarily the Selous Scouts and the RLI, and were without doubt instrumental in forcing President Samora Machel to apply similar pressure on Robert Mugabe.

The political backdrop to this final round of the war was this: soon after the election of the first black Rhodesian prime minister, Bishop Abel Muzorewa, and the implementation of the internal settlement, a Conservative government was elected into power in Britain, headed by arch conservative Margaret Thatcher.

Thatcher's victory injected a tremendous amount of optimism into the hearts of those white Rhodesians remaining committed to the country, and there certainly was a bias within the new establishment at Whitehall to reward Zimbabwe–Rhodesia with recognition. Soon after her inauguration, however, and a few weeks

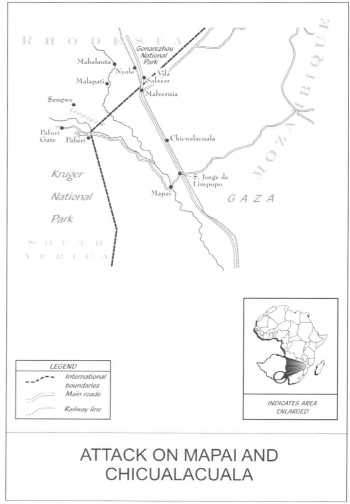

ATTACK ON MAPAI AND CHICUALACUALA

Source Genevieve Edwards

prior to a pivotal Commonwealth heads of government meeting due to be held in Lusaka in August of 1979, notice was served on her by virtually every member of the Commonwealth committee, and in particular Nigeria, that any substantive move toward recognizing a settlement in Rhodesia that did not include the two members of the Patriotic Front—Robert Mugabe and Joshua Nkomo—would invite mutiny within the Commonwealth.[*]

Confronted with this, Margaret Thatcher had no choice but to concede in her keynote speech that, although Britain had every intention of recognizing Rhodesian independence, it would not

---

* In May 1979 it was announced by Nigerian military leader Olusegun Obasanjo that Nigerian public contracts would henceforth be denied to British firms. This moratorium would remain in effect until such time as majority rule was established in Rhodesia. In July, Shell-BP Nigeria was nationalized in protest against the sale of Nigerian petroleum to South Africa. The Nigerian government then dumped £500 million sterling on the international currency exchanges in order first to destabilize sterling and secondly to dispel any doubts about Nigeria's determination and regional economic clout.

A SAAF Puma transporting troops during Operation Uric.
Source Neill Jackson

be under the current constitution, and not within the terms of the internal settlement as it stood. The power that the white minority enjoyed to block any undesirable amendment to the constitution was disproportionate to their demographic representation. This rendered the internal settlement defective in the view of the British government.

Grasping the moment, a majority of Commonwealth leaders urged the British prime minister to convene a constitutional conference during which the current internal settlement could be reworked and expanded to include the Patriotic Front, since, quite obviously, Muzorewa's government lacked the authenticity of genuine black power. White abhorrence toward dealing with Mugabe and Nkomo would have to be overcome.

On 10 September 1979, negotiations between all parties in the Rhodesian conflict got underway at Lancaster House in London,

chaired by British Foreign Secretary Lord Carrington, and seen by the British as the last roll of the dice in the long and bitter saga of post-UDI Rhodesia. The heads of delegations were Bishop Abel Muzorewa for the government of Zimbabwe-Rhodesia, Robert Mugabe for ZANU and Joshua Nkomo for ZAPU. Among these three, the first among equals was without doubt Robert Mugabe, before whose aggressive and belligerent negotiation style both Nkomo and Muzorewa wilted. Smith attended as a member of Muzorewa's delegation, and although he too displayed a great deal of aggression and intransigence, his was not the authoritative position. In fact the white man most feared at the conference was Lieutenant-General Peter Walls, who was summoned to the conference late in October, and whose unenviable job it was to choreograph the curtain call of white Rhodesia both at the conference itself and on the battlefield.

As the conference was convening the dust was settling on the penultimate Rhodesian operation in Mozambique, Operation Uric, which, over the first week of September 1979, combined waves of air and ground assaults on selected targets up the length of the Limpopo valley that severely disrupted communications between Maputo and the Frelimo and ZANLA forward bases near the Rhodesian border. On 6 September an assault on the main base at Mapai quickly deteriorated into intense and bloody trench fighting. As the day wore on, RLI ground units were forced to swallow the unprecedented humiliation of having their attack beaten off by an inferior enemy. A South African Puma helicopter carrying 17 people took a direct hit from an RPG-7 rocket that killed all on board. Army units despatched to investigate found the wreckage and the bodies, and assumed that they would be recovered once Mapai had successfully been taken.

Support Commando 1RLI elements assemble at Ruda, Honde valley, on the Mozambican border for Operation Miracle.

Artillery barrage on 'Monte Cassino'—veteran 25-pounders in action during Operation Miracle.

A Bell 'Huey' (Cheetah in RhAF parlance) uplifting captured weapons during mop-up operations after Operation Miracle.

Mapai remained untaken, and the bodies unrecovered. Although dramatic, and extremely destructive on the Mozambican transport infrastructure running up the Limpopo valley, the operation was not deemed to have been a success. A relatively low kill ratio of 20:1 (300 ZANLA/Frelimo dead to 15 Rhodesian personnel) fell some way below the acquired average, and certainly below what would be sustainable. Nonetheless, politically, the message was delivered and Robert Mugabe came under even greater pressure from Mozambique to bring an end to the war

Later that month, the point was reinforced by a second combined operation, spearheaded by the Selous Scouts and supported by the RhAF and units of the RLI. The operation was codenamed Miracle, and targeted ZANLA facilities that had been re-established near Chimoio in Mozambique in the aftermath of Operation Dingo. Operation Miracle was the closest to a conventional operation that the Rhodesians ever attempted. It involved a large and heavily armed column supported by artillery, mortars and air strikes, targeting a sprawling ZANLA base facility that had been deliberately spaced over a large area to inhibit any attempt at the favoured Fire Force style of assault.

This operation was undoubtedly successful, but again the cost was high. Two RhAF airmen and an RLI officer and a member of the Selous Scouts had been killed along with the devastating loss of hardware in the form of a Canberra bomber, a ground attack Hawker Hunter, a Bell 205 helicopter and an Alouette helicopter. None of this was sustainable in the long term and should matters in London not conclude in a favourable end to the war, Rhodesia could hardly be expected to sustain such losses for much longer.

In the meanwhile, as the dust settled in Mozambique, and a chastened Robert Mugabe negotiated under pressure from his sponsors, the SAS had been hard at work in Zambia attempting to checkmate ZIPRA ambitions to launch a conventional attack against Rhodesia, while at the same time sending a similar message to Kenneth Kaunda that the price of supporting and providing succour to the enemies of Rhodesia would be very high indeed.

Operation Cheese was arguably one of the most daring, innovative and desperate operations of the entire war. Early in October 1979, a four-man SAS freefall pathfinder team was flown into Zambia aboard the legendary Jack Malloch's Douglas DC-7, and inserted at a point near Chandesi in northern Zambia, some 600 kilometres as the crow flies from the nearest point of the Rhodesian frontier.* The target was a bridge over the Chambeshi river that served the TanZam rail link between Kapiri Mposhi in Zambia and Dar es Salaam, which would disrupt Zambian export and force a greater reliance on rail routes through Rhodesia. Once the target area had been reconnoitred, a second twelve-man team was inserted, and the bridge was successfully blown. Exit was improvised through the hijack of a haulage vehicle that was used to transport the SAS team and equipment southward toward the South Luangwa National Park, and within range of helicopter extraction.

The Rhodesian security forces did not experience a single tactical defeat at any time during the war, but there were occasions, such as during Operation Uric, when an operational objective was not achieved for one reason or another, and a tactical withdrawal ordered, but this was rare. One occasion was Operation Tepid.

Throughout October multiple threads of intelligence were coalescing to suggest that ZPIRA was assembling conventional forces and equipment in Zambia in readiness for a major push into Rhodesia, no doubt to pre-empt a ZANLA military victory or a disadvantageous conclusion for ZAPU in the ongoing Lancaster House conference in London. ZIPRA was relatively poorly represented in the field at that time, which contrasted to a strong ZANLA presence in most areas. Clearly something needed to be done quickly in order to check the ability of ZIPRA to move large amount of force toward the Rhodesian border.

The obvious strategy for a hostile land invasion against Rhodesia would be a simultaneous assault on the three key access points into Rhodesia—the Victoria Falls bridge, Kariba dam wall and the Chirundu bridge, located some thirty miles north of Kariba.

It had been reported that MiG-21 fighters, alongside much other heavy ordnance, had begun to arrive in Zambia. These

---

* Jack Malloch was a maverick aviator and Rhodesian sanctions-buster. He served in the RAF alongside Ian Smith during the Second World War, and then later flew in various capacities as a gun runner and agent for hire, ultimately forming the lynchpin of Rhodesian sanctions-busting enterprise throughout the war period.

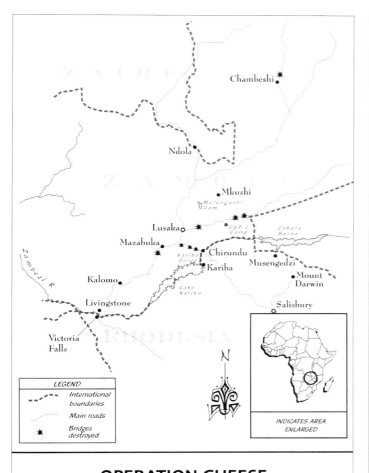

OPERATION CHEESE
BRIDGES DESTROYED – ZAMBIA

Source Genevieve Edwards

SANCTION-BUSTING FLIGHTS

With his DC-7 Jack Malloch was a legendary sanctions-buster during the war years. *Source Genevieve Edwards*

were superior to anything that the Rhodesians were flying, and with air superiority over the region, a bridgehead could easily be established on the Rhodesian side, and after securing the two airports at Kariba and Victoria Falls, large Libyan transporters could then start bringing in troops and equipment.

In that event the game would be lost. Rhodesians would have no choice but to drop their own bridges if there was to be any chance of forestalling an invasion, and even that would not automatically limit any movement across the Zambezi.

Operation Tepid was a combined RLI–SAS operation intended to neutralize a ZIPRA position situated about fifteen miles northwest of Siavonga, the sister town to Kariba on the northern side of the dam wall. Earlier in the year Rhodesian aircraft had registered anti-aircraft fire from two ridges located on either side of a salt pan where it was later established by an SAS reconnaissance patrol that a large ZIPRA detachment was in situ.

The attack went in at dawn on 20 October but quickly came up against a confident, well-trained and heavily armed ZIPRA force. Outgunned and unable to make headway, attacking troops were forced to rely on waves of airborne rocket and missile attacks that also achieved very little. The operation was successful only insofar as ZIPRA effected an orderly withdrawal from their

positions under cover of a heavy mortar bombardment, losing only a handful of men during the entire operation, at the cost of one RLI member.

The final operation in this series was Operation Dice, an SAS demolition operation, supported by the RLI, and planned to knock out key bridges and culverts along the Great East Road from Lusaka to Malawi, and the southern and southwestern routes from the capital to Chirundu and Livingstone respectively.

As the final details of the Lancaster House agreement were drafted, nine Zambian bridges were demolished, somewhat gratuitously as it would turn out, since a ceasefire was shortly thereafter declared, after which Kenneth Kaunda forbade any heavy ZIPRA troop movements, or indeed any mobilizations whatsoever.

Nonetheless, there was a certain satisfaction on the part of the Rhodesians in delivering this valedictory blow before all sides took a step back and prepared themselves for the last phase of the war, and a de facto political conclusion to a heroic, if somewhat misguided defence of white rule in southern Africa. From that point onward responsibility for turning out the lights fell to the politicians. Apart from a few forlorn notions of reigniting the war, the enterprise of Rhodesia was over.

CHAPTER FOURTEEN:
THE UNBEARABLE TRUTH

You must remember, this is Africa. This isn't Little Puddleton-on-the-Marsh, and they behave differently here. They think nothing of sticking tent poles up each other's whatnot, and doing filthy, beastly things to each other. It does happen, I'm afraid. It's a very wild thing, an election
— Lord Soames, British Governor of Rhodesia, 1979

In the rotating lore of counter-insurgency and liberation struggle there is a record of an apocryphal exchange between US Colonel Harry G. Summers and North Vietnamese Colonel Tu during the tense negotiations that followed the collapse of the South Vietnamese government. "You know, you never defeated us on the battlefield." Summers is said to have remarked, to which Tu replied. "That may be so, but it is also irrelevant."

American troops returning to the United States could hardly have felt the concentrated sense of frustration and betrayal that the ignoble end to the Rhodesian war inspired in the fighting men of Rhodesia. It hardly impacted the deep emotions felt by a generation of white Rhodesian youth to be told that the defence of white hegemony in Africa had always been an anachronism, and was always doomed to fail. The war had been fought primarily by young men who fought it on a visceral level, and the deaths of comrades and the waste of life inspired the grief that might be expected in any similar circumstance, and likewise a deep-seated urge not to let go of a lost cause.

The Lancaster House conference resulted in a proposed constitution that amounted to a defeat for white Rhodesia. A free and fair, all-party election more or less guaranteed Robert Mugabe victory, and while there was a certain amount of wishful thinking that the lacklustre and powerless Bishop Abel Muzorewa might sneak an electoral victory, or that some sort of a coalition with the less fearsome Joshua Nkomo might head off a Mugabe coup, in reality no one really held out any hope that Mugabe could be effectively checkmated without a military coup of some sort.

On 11 December 1979, a British governor in the form of Lord Christopher Soames arrived in Rhodesia as a symbol of the colony's return to legality, after which the process of campaigning for the all-party election began.

Soames had been given a difficult task. There had been an understanding reached between the British and the Rhodesians, specifically between Lieutenant-General Peter Walls and Lord Peter Carrington, British foreign secretary, and chairman of the Lancaster House conference, that a direct line of communication would be maintained between the general and the British prime minister throughout the electoral process, and that any sign of campaign malfeasance on the part of any party would result in the removal of that party from the ballot.

In the event, voter intimidation was rampant. Part of the ceasefire agreement had been that all active guerrilla units within Rhodesia would gather at a number of assembly points to await the outcome of the election while the Rhodesian Army would be confined to barracks. ZANLA in particular, with the largest concentration of force within Rhodesia, maintained its main force in the field by handing outdated weaponry to non-combatant youth to represent numbers at the assembly points. Thus large numbers of active cadres mingled with the population, representing a strong presence to black voters in the countryside in order to remind them that a failure to support the party would mean an immediate return to war. Such had been the level of terrorization applied in years past that no reminder was necessary of what that would practically mean.

The British, through Lord Soames, where aware of this, but a combination of their unwillingness to antagonize a manifestly belligerent and dangerous Robert Mugabe, with the risk that would run of collapsing the entire agreement, and a recognition that even in the absence of widespread intimidation, Mugabe would in all likelihood win anyway, caused them to turn a blind eye and allow the process to continue regardless.

Walls, in the meanwhile, was confronted by an unenviable decision: to react or not to react. Local security concerns had been presented to him in two intelligence papers that had been prepared by senior security force officers.

The first of these listed a series of possible actions to oppose and prevent a ZANU or ZAPU victory. It was understood, or perhaps more accurately, it was hoped, that the result of the election would be a narrow victory for Mugabe, which could conceivably be countered by a coalition of Joshua Nkomo's ZAPU, Abel Muzorewa's UANC and Ian Smith's Rhodesian Front (later renamed the Conservative Alliance of Zimbabwe).

The second paper warned of a worst-case scenario: a likely outright electoral victory by Robert Mugabe. In this case the potential for a euphoric rush to the capital by victorious guerrilla groups, supported by allied civilians, was very high. Various actions were suggested to prevent or protect against this.

These intelligence reports, however, as fanciful as they were, along with a general sense of anxiety felt within the security circles and the wider white society, were more than likely what lay behind the formulation of a military plan, codenamed Operation Quartz.

Operation Quartz envisaged a plan to quickly neutralize ZANU's main force concentrations that were conveniently contained, for the most part, in a number of assembly points. The understanding that underwrote the plan was in essence that Mugabe would react upon losing the election, or being outmanoeuvred upon a narrow victory, by attempting some sort of a rapid armed takeover, or at the very least a quick return to war. ZANLA positions, including a temporary senior command

Lieutenant-General Peter Walls.

British Foreign Secretary Lord Peter Carrington.

A ZIPRA guerrilla poses in his trench at an assembly point.

HQ that had been located in the grounds of the University of Rhodesia, would be attacked and wiped out by a combination of Rhodesian ground and air forces. South African assistance would also be provided in the form of helicopters and a small detachment of the South African Reconnaissance Regiment. South African troops were likewise to be deployed in the strategic area around Beitbridge to protect the rearguard of a potential white exodus to South Africa should matters turn ugly in Rhodesia.

Operation Hectic was an allied plan that involved the direct assassination of Mugabe and his key aids, with Nkomo also targeted, but not quite so comprehensively. The operation was to be carried out by the elite troops of the Rhodesian SAS. And in fact a series of attempts on Mugabe's life was made during the tense weeks running up to the ballot, but each time he managed to slip through the net, either as a consequence of good luck or prior warning from somewhere.

The fact that Mugabe did seem to be consistently warned of any threat to his life tended to prompt renewed speculation regarding the existence of a mole at the highest security level in the country. A name quite often mentioned in this regard has been that of Ken Flower, local intelligence supremo and Director General of the powerful Central Intelligence Organization.

Flower wrote a highly detailed account of his years at the helm of Rhodesian intelligence, *Serving Secretly*, but failed to mention Operation Quartz. Nothing has ever been proven against Flower, however, who died in 1987, and who continues to enjoy the support of many ex-Rhodesian intelligence and security force members who do not accept that there is any truth in accusations against him.

The fact remains, however, that a number of unsuccessful assassination attempts were made against both Mugabe and Nkomo by different units and agencies, each of which was frustrated, suggesting very strongly a very highly placed intelligence leak.

One of a number of exceedingly unpalatable aspects of Operation Hectic involved a smear campaign against Mugabe and ZANU, with attempts to blow up churches in and around Salisbury for the purpose of blaming guerrilla elements and their atavistic, anti-Christian–Marxist ideological leanings. In another highly dubious operation, a wedding party of ostensible UANC supporters travelling in a bus between Umtali and Salisbury was ambushed with many killed. The operation was apparently undertaken by rogue elements of the Selous Scouts, however no definitive proof of this has ever been presented. The apparent objective of this attack was to suggest that it had been staged by vengeful ZANLA elements. A bomb attack was also staged against the printing facilities of Moto Press, the publisher of a popular black readership magazine, after a spurious edition of the publication hit the streets of Salisbury painting a distorted picture of Robert Mugabe. The bomb attack was intended to be interpreted as a ZANLA retaliation, which was confused somewhat by the discovery at the scene of a white male corpse with South African money in his pocket.

In the meanwhile, the main attack force that was earmarked to assault the various ZANLA assembly points combined the RhAF, units of the Rhodesia Light Infantry, the SAS and Selous Scouts, supported by South African special forces and paratroopers. Ten targets were identified. These were assembly points Alpha, Bravo, Charlie, Delta, Echo, Foxtrot, Golf, Hotel, Juliet and Kilo. ZIPRA was not specifically targeted—Nkomo was to be a pivotal alliance member in a new government—although assembly points Kilo and Juliet were shared by both ZIPRA and ZANLA. The urban assault on the ZANLA HQ would be carried out by units of the SAS

A female cadre. Women guerrillas were fearsome adversaries and much respected by the RLI.

supported by tanks and armoured cars of the Rhodesian Armoured Car Regiment, with the addition of 106mm recoilless rifles.

The Rhodesian Army fielded primarily South Africa Eland armoured cars, a close variant of the French Panhard AML. This was a versatile platform armed with either with a 90mm quick-firing low-pressure gun or a 60mm breech-loading mortar, the former most commonly. These had superseded a fleet of British Ferret armoured cars that had never seen a great deal of active service in the war, and were by 1980 largely obsolete. In addition, the Rhodesians had acquired eight Russian T-55 tanks in October 1979, part of a consignment of weapons seized by the South Africans from a French cargo vessel believed to be transporting weapons to Angola, then more or less at war with South Africa.

Other military, police and auxiliary units, although not earmarked for use against the targeted assembly points, were nonetheless placed on standby for rapid deployment to areas of strategic importance, and for the general defence and protection of key sites and population centres. Various signals were sent to local JOCs and sub-JOCs, briefing them on what roles they were to play in the upcoming operation. Copies of these have been preserved, against orders, by some of the officers thus detailed, and a number of these are now in the possession of the Rhodesian Army Association. The illustrated examples were provided by Captain Peter Bray of the RhACR.

It can be seen from these orders that the territorial battalions and independent companies, alongside various Support Unit and SFA units, were to be concentrated in strategic and vulnerable areas throughout the Operation Thrasher area (primarily), which was the principal ZANLA theatre, and the area most likely to be affected by an emptying of the ZANLA assembly points. An indication is given by this of the extent to which the matter was taken seriously by the military high command and the various JOCs.

The signal for the start of Operation Quartz, however, was never issued. Robert Mugabe and his ZANU won an unexpected, but in retrospect inevitable majority at

An RLI armoured column on the road near Nyamapanda during the aborted Operation Quartz in which the Rhodesian security forces were to take out ZANLA and ZIPRA assembly points.

the polls. The Rhodesian military machine, primed and ready for the signal, waited in breathless anticipation. Three hours before the anticipated launch of the operation, however, it was cancelled.

Many reasons have been cited for this. The first was the belief of the commanding officer of the SAS, Lieutenant-Colonel Garth Barrett, commanding the pivotal unit in the entire plan, that the operation had been compromised at the highest planning level. This again implies a sense of unease about the existence of a well-placed mole in the system. The SAS had been thwarted several times in efforts to kill Mugabe so there was certainly some basis for this fear.

Another theory put forward was that the close proximity of some ZIPRA and ZANLA elements had precipitated an inevitable leak of information. A third and more plausible explanation was that General Walls himself, head of ComOps and the last substantive Rhodesian white man on the inside of the ceasefire negotiation process, recognized that the extent of Robert Mugabe's win nullified any real chance of a coup succeeding. Quartz had been formulated on the understanding that Mugabe would not win, or at least would not win resoundingly, and when he did it seemed that an inevitable course of action had begun that could now not reasonably be halted.

It has also been suggested that Walls never intended there to be any kind of violent Rhodesian effort to reclaim power. The planning and dissemination of the details of the plan were simply to forestall any maverick individual action on the part of units or commanders acting in the belief that victory was being handed to the enemy. If it was generally believed within the armed forces that a centralized scheme was in place then individual units and battalions would be likely to remain under orders.

Even after the Mugabe victory had been announced some expectation lingered that a coup of some sort would be ordered. This did not entirely evaporate until Walls appeared on national television and addressed the nation with the stern warning that "anybody who gets out of line or for whatever reason starts

disobeying the law will be dealt with effectively and swiftly ..."

Interestingly, Lieutenant-General Peter Walls was careful to distance himself from the planning of Operation Quartz. This is quite understandable, bearing in mind that at the time he was walking a tightrope between ushering in majority rule and ushering out a highly motivated, aggressive and effective military machine that certainly did not deserve defeat in terms of its battlefield performance.

It might be remembered that Rhodesian ex-prime minister Ian Smith had not represented the Zimbabwe–Rhodesia government during the Lancaster House negotiations, Bishop Abel Muzorewa by then being prime minister. It had been Walls who had appeared at the conference as the white man in Rhodesia to deal with, notwithstanding the fact that a number of white members of government served on the Zimbabwe–Rhodesia negotiating team.

Walls could hardly then openly acknowledge Operation Quartz, bearing in mind that he was actively trying to win the trust of the incoming government, being, at the very least, the titular head of the armed forces integration. This did not last very long and Walls quickly fell from grace with the incoming ZANU government, as did Ian Smith, and the process of sweeping white influence out of government and the armed forces soon claimed both.

Walls was in fact accused of treason in parliament by the then minister of information Nathan Shamuyarira, claiming that: 1) Operation Quartz involved a military takeover of the country scheduled for 4 March, the day of Mugabe's election victory, and 2) ZANLA troops had been purposely massed in assembly points in order that the Rhodesian Air Force could deal with them in concentration.

ZIPRA was not to be attacked in the hope of promoting an alliance between Nkomo and Muzorewa once ZANLA had been neutralized. Operation Quartz was cancelled a bare three hours before it was due to be launched, because Walls felt that it could not succeed in view of Mugabe's overwhelming victory at the polls.

All of this Walls denied, but was not believed, and he was advised soon afterward by members of the government to leave the country without delay. In conclusion it can hardly be credible that the commander of the armed forces of Rhodesia could have been unaware of an operation that required such a widespread mobilization of the armed forces, and an action likely to generate tremendous hostility overseas and an enormous political embarrassment to the government of the United Kingdom. This in particular bearing in mind that the government then lay under

Preparing for Operation Quartz.

the ostensible control of a British governor, meaning that war thereafter would not be with white Rhodesia, but with Britain.

However it has been stated by a brigade major of 3 Brigade based in Umtali that Walls might not have been aware of the precise codeword 'Quartz' because this was a codeword specific to the mobilization of 3 Brigade in terms of the actions planned for the operation (1 Brigade Bulawayo being supplied with the codeword 'Melrose'). This is not to imply that Walls was unaware of the operation as such.

However, whatever the facts of Operation Quartz, the operation that never was, independence was celebrated at midnight on 18 April 1980. The Rhodesian Green and White had by then already been consigned to history, so it was the lowering of the Union Jack that preceded the hoisting of the new Zimbabwe Green, Red, Black and Gold. A flyover of a single Canberra bomber concluded the official ceremony. As he approached the stadium the pilot opened the bomb bay. The Canberra was configured so that the slipstream created by the open bomb doors caused an otherworldly howl that was all too familiar to those who had been bombed in the past by this old warhorse. The RAR, who never had, kept their ranks, but the ZIPRA and ZANLA men both on the field and in the stands dived for cover.

With that valedictory reminder of who had won the shooting war, Rhodesia disappeared into history. Soon after the election the various territorial units were disarmed and disbanded. All the aircraft of the Rhodesian Air Force were recalled to the main bases of Thornhill in Gwelo and New Sarum in Salisbury to await the new military command. The Rhodesian Light Infantry was disbanded as a unit on 1 November 1980, although by then the cream of the unit had left the country. A few remaining officers and troops would assist in the formation and training of the new Zimbabwe National Army (ZNA).

The famous RLI 'Troopie' statue was smuggled out of the country, along with other treasures of the regiment, while the regimental colours were hung in the Anglican Cathedral in Salisbury. The Trooper statue now stands on the grounds of Hatfield House, country seat of the Marquess of Salisbury, where it was re-dedicated on 28 September 2008

The Rhodesian African Rifles was disbanded soon after independence and was integrated into 1, 3 and 4 Brigades of the Zimbabwe National Army.

The SAS was withdrawn from the field and confined to barracks at the Kabrit Base, although by April 1980, the majority of its members had followed Lieutenant-Colonel Garth Barrett to South Africa where they reformed as 6 Recce Commando. On 31 December 1980 the unit was disbanded entirely. At a ceremony on 13 December the unit was addressed by its commanding officer, Major Grahame Wilson—the most decorated member of the security forces—who spoke to the remainder of his troops for the last time. "We will leave here not only in sorrow but filled with pride, dignity and honour in ourselves and in 1SAS. We have much to be grateful for."

The Selous Scouts more or less disappeared the moment that news filtered out that Mugabe had won the election. Those in the field were brought in, the peripheral bases were shut down and the regulars confined to the fort at Inkomo Barracks. 'Turned' guerrillas were now largely stranded, and of course had much to fear. Many white operatives followed the surviving C Squadron SAS members to South Africa where they were absorbed into the Recce Commandos.

In the intervening years the Rhodesian war has undergone an enormous amount of study and analysis, and the conclusion has been generally reached that, deep in the African hinterland, an extraordinary military phenomenon played out in the 1970s, that was as magnificent as it was improbable. That Rhodesia was attempting to defend the indefensible—both morally and militarily—is irrelevant to the fact that an astonishing fight was fought. Bearing in mind multiple equipment constraints, manpower shortages and ongoing political fetters, the forces opposing Rhodesia never stood a chance of an outright military victory. It was simply never feasible. This amounts to a triumph of military organization and strategy quite as much as unit-level commitment to the fight, and that fact has by now been widely acknowledged, but this is only half of the story.

The war did not really begin in earnest until Robert Mugabe was free to organize and plan, and the conclusion of the war was as much a vindication of his style of warfare as the Rhodesian resistance was to theirs. What Mugabe sought to achieve, he achieved. A military victory in the classic sense of the word was not necessary. The Rhodesians simply had to be pressured to the point of collapse. The ZANLA war was a test case of its kind, an African interpretation of people's war, and it was successful.

Both of these perspectives are equally true, which is what makes the Rhodesian war, or the Zimbabwe liberation struggle, such an enduringly fascinating subject, and the last word on the subject is a long way from being written.

Peter Baxter is an author, amateur historian and African field, mountain and heritage travel guide. Born in Kenya and educated in Zimbabwe, he has lived and travelled over much of southern and central Africa. He has guided in all the major mountain ranges south of the equator, helping develop the concept of sustainable travel, and the touring of battlefield and heritage sites in East Africa. Peter lives in Oregon, USA, working on the marketing of African heritage travel as well as a variety of book projects. His interests include British Imperial history in Africa and the East Africa campaign of the First World War in particular. His first book was *Rhodesia: Last Outpost of the British Empire*; he has written several books in the Africa@War series, including *France in Centrafrique*, *Selous Scouts*, *Mau Mau*, *Somalia* and *SAAF's Border War*.